Getting Started with Microsoft Lync Server 2013

Everything you need for understanding and working with Lync 2013 in a fast-paced manner

Fabrizio Volpe

BIRMINGHAM - MUMBAI

Getting Started with Microsoft Lync Server 2013

First published: July 2013

Production Reference: 1100713

Published by Packt Publishing Ltd.
Livery Place
35 Livery Street
Birmingham B3 2PB, UK.

ISBN 978-1-78217-993-1

www.packtpub.com

Cover Image by Massimiliano Mirri (info@maxmirriphotos.com)

Credits

Author
Fabrizio Volpe

Reviewers
Johan Veldhuis

Wang wei

Acquisition Editor
Kevin Colaco

Commissioning Editors
Ameya Sawant

Neha Nagwekar

Sharvari Tawde

Technical Editors
Jalasha D'costa

Krishnaveni Haridas

Amit Ramadas

Copy Editors
Aditya Nair

Alfida Paiva

Laxmi Subramanian

Project Coordinator
Siddhant Shetty

Proofreader
Clyde Jenkins

Indexer
Rekha Nair

Graphics
Abhinash Sahu

Production Coordinator
Prachali Bhiwandkar

Cover Work
Prachali Bhiwandkar

About the Author

Fabrizio Volpe has been working with the Iccrea Banking Group since 2000, as a network and systems administrator.

He is part of the Microsoft Technologies workgroup in Iccrea Banca, managing more than 2000 users at their central site, a nationwide network of branch offices, and providing services for more than 400 banks.

Since 2011, he has been awarded MVP on Directory Services from Microsoft, and is focused on Windows systems and security, unified communication, and virtualization.

Prior to the Iccrea Group, Fabrizio has collaborated with various IT companies, focused on Windows, security, networking, and messaging / unified communication products.

Since 2000, he has presented many events and conferences (Italian and international ones).

Fabrizio is committed to create contents that are accessible to a wide number of people, so he publishes content really often on SlideShare (`http://www.slideshare.net/fabriziov`), on his Lync2013 channel on YouTube (`http://www.youtube.com/user/lync2013`), and on his personal blog (`http://blog.lync2013.org`).

Acknowledgments

This work is dedicated to my son Federico and to my wife Antonella. You have made me stronger, better, and more fulfilled than I could have ever imagined.

I want to thank all the people at Packt Publishing for giving me the opportunity to write this book, and for all their great work on the long road from drafting to publishing.

I would like to express my gratitude to Susan S. Bradley (Senior Project Manager at Microsoft), to Johan Veldhuis (Exchange MVP), and to Wang wei (Lync MVP) for their help and support.

I would like to extend my heartfelt thanks to the people at Gruppo Need (http://www.grupponeed.it/) for their incredible assistance, allowing me to use the hardware, infrastructure, and tech support from the labs I used during the preparation of the book, for free.

About the Reviewers

Johan Veldhuis is a Technical Consultant who works at a consultancy firm that specializes in Microsoft Unified Communications solutions. In that role, he is responsible for designing, implementing, migrating, and troubleshooting Microsoft UC solutions.

In 2007, he started to blog actively about Exchange and assist people on several fora. This resulted in an Exchange Server MVP award in 2009, which he's held on to ever since. Besides his own blog on his website (`www.johanveldhuis.nl`), Johan has been a regular author for Simple-Talk (`www.simple-talk.com`) and several other blogs.

Besides blogging, Johan is a member of *The UC Architects* (`www.theucarchitects.com`), which is a bi-weekly Podcast, where Exchange and Lync freaks discuss both Exchange- and Lync-related topics.

Wang wei is the principal Systems Engineer with Sonus. He has been in the IT industry for the past 10 years. As a Systems Engineer, he specializes in Lync voices architecture, media gateway, and SBC solution. As a Microsoft Lync MVP, he enjoys sharing his findings on Lync in the community. When not playing with technology, he spends time with his wife and kid in Chengdu. He enjoys good food and hanging out with friends.

www.PacktPub.com

Support files, eBooks, discount offers and more

You might want to visit www.PacktPub.com for support files and downloads related to your book.

Did you know that Packt offers eBook versions of every book published, with PDF and ePub files available? You can upgrade to the eBook version at www.PacktPub.com and as a print book customer, you are entitled to a discount on the eBook copy. Get in touch with us at service@packtpub.com for more details.

At www.PacktPub.com, you can also read a collection of free technical articles, sign up for a range of free newsletters and receive exclusive discounts and offers on Packt books and eBooks.

http://PacktLib.PacktPub.com

Do you need instant solutions to your IT questions? PacktLib is Packt's online digital book library. Here, you can access, read and search across Packt's entire library of books.

Why Subscribe?

- Fully searchable across every book published by Packt
- Copy and paste, print and bookmark content
- On demand and accessible via web browser

Free Access for Packt account holders

If you have an account with Packt at www.PacktPub.com, you can use this to access PacktLib today and view nine entirely free books. Simply use your login credentials for immediate access.

Instant Updates on New Packt Books

Get notified! Find out when new books are published by following @PacktEnterprise on Twitter, or the *Packt Enterprise* Facebook page.

Table of Contents

Preface

Lync 2013 is really hard to describe in a few words. We are talking about a product that enables users to perform instant messaging, audio conferencing, and video conferencing. This product features Enterprise Voice that includes the capability to integrate itself with legacy PSTN and PBX through a gateway. We are able to grant access to external users via the Internet in a secure manner, and they will have a Lync experience not different from the one users have in an internal network. Such richness with regard to features and such flexibility makes Lync 2013 a game changer in the world of unified communication (UC). If we are going to deploy a new office in a "green field" situation, if we need to replace an old telephony infrastructure, if we want to enable our users to "anywhere" access for audio and video conferencing, or if we are evaluating a cloud solution for a part of our company or branch offices, the answer to all these different situations may always be Lync.

The strong integration with existing Active Directory, Exchange, and SharePoint deployments implies that a lot of IT professionals who were not interested in the UC world before, are now involved in the deployment, design, and management of Lync. Also, people who already have a good experience with other solutions, will be increasingly interested in Lync as a potential solution to add to their toolbox. And that is why this book exists. If you need to get started with Lync 2013, or there are some features that you would like to know better, I hope that you find your answer here.

What this book covers

Chapter 1, *Installing a Lync 2013 Enterprise Pool*, introduces the basic concepts of Lync 2013, and explains in a step-by-step manner the deployment of an Enterprise pool of Lync.

Chapter 2, *Understanding Front End Pool Pairing*, explores Front End pairing, which is a new feature of Lync 2013, that enables a high level of resiliency using different servers that may have been deployed (also) on different sites. In this chapter, we will see what pool pairing is and how to configure it.

Chapter 3, *Deploying Lync Mobility*, demonstrates mobility as one of the most requested and interesting features of Lync 2013. This chapter explains how to enable external users on Lync, and how to support mobile devices.

Chapter 4, *Integrating Lync Mediation Server*, explains why whenever we are going to deploy Enterprise Voice, the first Lync role we need is the Mediation Server. This is a function that has an enormous impact on our design and implementation, and we will try to deeply dive into it during the chapter.

Chapter 5, *Getting Started with Lync Enterprise Voice*, introduces all the basic concepts and tasks required to deploy a VoIP solution with Lync 2013 inside our company. Although the topic is really massive, the ideas presented here will give the base to start working with Enterprise Voice.

Chapter 6, *Deploying Persistent Chat Server*, introduces Persistent Chat, which is a new feature of Lync 2013, that enables the creation of a knowledge base for your users and the construction of "private" spaces, where a selected groups of our users are able to communicate. Here we will see how it works and how it is implemented.

Chapter 7, *Choosing Lync 2013 Clients*, focusses on knowing all the existing clients, their characteristics, and limits as a fundamental step to design the right solution and to achieve the best result for you users with the least effort. Here we will explore the different available solutions.

What you need for this book

To deploy Lync 2013 in our internal network, we will need Windows 2008 R2 or Windows 2012, the Lync 2013 installation media, and the Office Web Apps setup. An Active Directory infrastructure is mandatory to install Lync, and it is useful to have an internal certification authority available. If we want to grant access to the external users, a reverse proxy solution (IIS, Apache, or any hardware or software enabled for publishing) is required, along with an additional Lync server dedicated to the Edge role. Also, in the aforementioned scenario, we will usually prefer to have an SSL certificate from a third-party authority.

Who this book is for

This book is for IT professionals who are involved in the design, maintenance, or deployment of a Lync 2013 environment, for unified communication professionals coming with an experience in solutions from different vendors, and for decision-makers and project managers who want to have an idea of the capabilities and technical requirements (and impact) of Lync.

Conventions

In this book, you will find a number of styles of text that distinguish between different kinds of information. Here are some examples of these styles, and an explanation of their meaning.

Code words in text are shown as follows: "Once up and running, the server generates three subfolders: `1-ApplicationServer-1`, `1-CentralMgmt-1`, and `1-Webservices-1`."

Any command-line input or output is written as follows:

```
Export-CsConfiguration -File C:\temp\export.zip
```

New terms and **important words** are shown in bold. Words that you see on the screen, in menus or dialog boxes for example, appear in the text like this: "We will select the **Import from a file** option."

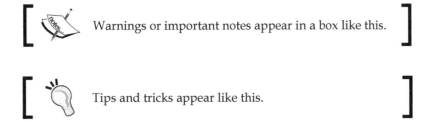

Warnings or important notes appear in a box like this.

Tips and tricks appear like this.

Reader feedback

Feedback from our readers is always welcome. Let us know what you think about this book—what you liked or may have disliked. Reader feedback is important for us to develop titles that you really get the most out of.

To send us general feedback, simply send an e-mail to `feedback@packtpub.com`, and mention the book title via the subject of your message.

If there is a topic that you have expertise and you are interested in either writing or contributing to a book, see our author guide on `www.packtpub.com/authors`.

Customer support

Now that you are the proud owner of a Packt book, we have a number of things to help you to get the most from your purchase.

Errata

Although we have taken every care to ensure the accuracy of our content, mistakes do happen. If you find a mistake in one of our books—maybe a mistake in the text or the code—we would be grateful if you would report this to us. By doing so, you can save other readers from frustration and help us improve subsequent versions of this book. If you find any errata, please report them by visiting http://www.packtpub.com/submit-errata, selecting your book, clicking on the **errata submission form** link, and entering the details of your errata. Once your errata are verified, your submission will be accepted and the errata will be uploaded on our website, or added to any list of existing errata, under the Errata section of that title. Any existing errata can be viewed by selecting your title from http://www.packtpub.com/support.

Piracy

Piracy of copyright material on the Internet is an ongoing problem across all media. At Packt, we take the protection of our copyright and licenses very seriously. If you come across any illegal copies of our works, in any form, on the Internet, please provide us with the location address or website name immediately so that we can pursue a remedy.

Please contact us at copyright@packtpub.com with a link to the suspected pirated material.

We appreciate your help in protecting our authors, and our ability to bring you valuable content.

Questions

You can contact us at questions@packtpub.com if you are having a problem with any aspect of the book, and we will do our best to address it.

1
Installing a Lync 2013 Enterprise Pool

This chapter will introduce some of the fundamentals of Lync 2013's working environment. Here we will also see a step-by-step setup of an Enterprise pool with a clear explanation of the logic of the different operations we will perform.

Lync Server roles

To understand what we are going to do, it is necessary to clarify some basic concepts along the way, starting with the Lync versions and available "roles".

A Lync deployment is made up of a variable number of servers (depending on the features we are going to use and the level of availability and security we need).

A part of these servers will not even have Lync installed, but it is mandatory to build the basic infrastructure.

The cornerstone for the entire organization is Lync Front End, made up of a **Standard Edition server** (**SE**) (a single box with all the features available locally), or by a pool made up of one or more Lync **Enterprise Edition server** (**EE**) units connected with three or more **Back End** Servers units (fundamentally one or more SQL Server databases).

The latter configuration will support scalability and **high availability** (**HA**), especially if we decide to use SQL mirroring, which now replaces the SQL clustering we had to use with Lync 2010.

There is no difference in the unified communication features we have with a Standard Edition and with an Enterprise Edition, but SE servers cannot be grouped in a pool; they can just be "paired" with each other (we will talk about Enterprise pools in the course of this chapter, and pairing will be covered in *Chapter 2, Understanding Front End Pool Pairing*).

From a server-licensing point of view, in Lync 2013 there is only a single "Lync" license, with no distinction between Standard Edition or Enterprise Edition. However, the difference still exists from the point of view of deployment. A **Client Access License** (**CAL**) is also required for the Lync users based on the features they will require. For the details on licensing, please refer to *Licensing Lync* at `http://office.microsoft.com/en-us/lync/microsoft-lync-licensing-overview-lync-for-multiple-users-FX103789668.aspx`.

A mandatory requirement for any Lync deployment is a pre-existing Active Directory infrastructure; so we take it as given to have a domain with directory services up and running.

In a small company that does not need to publish Lync on the Internet, a single Standard Edition server (and a domain controller) is all we need to be able to deliver Lync to our users, because almost all the services are installed locally (PowerPoint presentation broadcasts require an additional Office Web Apps server. See *Web Conferencing Overview* at `http://technet.microsoft.com/en-us/library/gg425913.aspx` for more information).

 Enterprise Voice may require additional hardware, depending on the kind of connection to the public telephony service that is made available.

Additional servers for external user access

If Lync services have to be available to the external users, we have to add a **Lync Edge** and a reverse proxy (to publish the web services of Lync).

 A detailed explanation of this topic will be included in *Chapter 3, Deploying Lync Mobility and External Users Access*.

Lync Edge

Edge is a Lync server designed to be connected to the Internet to extend Lync services outside an internal network with no VPN or a dedicated connection. Lync Edge can be deployed in a pool for high availability.

Reverse proxy

A reverse proxy is required for external access. For more information, you may refer to the previously mentioned *Chapter 3*, and to the *Setting Up Reverse Proxy Servers* article at http://technet.microsoft.com/en-us/library/gg398069.aspx.

Continuity for the services published with the reverse proxy requires a specific hardware or software solution, depending on the kind of server we are using to publish Lync.

Also, if there are existing deployments without a reverse proxy, publishing Lync services directly to the Internet will not be a supported solution. In the following diagram, we can see a high-level overview of the previously mentioned scenarios:

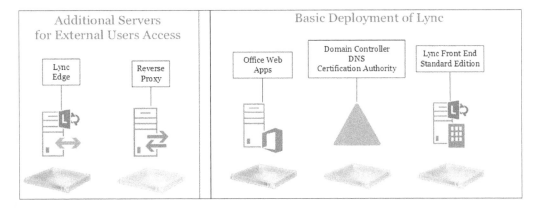

To complete the list of Lync roles, we must also consider the following areas:

- **Mediation**: This can be deployed as a separate server or collocated on a Front End. It is used for IP-PBX, Gateway, and SBC interoperability to provide Enterprise Voice and dial-in conferencing.

- **Director**: This server enhances the performance of user authentication and adds a security layer.

- **Persistent Chat Server**: This server is used to create one or more "chat rooms" that can be moderated, and to retain the instant messages of the users for a defined amount of time.

- **Monitoring**: This role, collocated on a Front End, collects data about the quality of the service with Enterprise Voice and audio/video conferencing.

- **Archiving**: This role, collocated on a Front End, is used for compliance; it stores IM messages and conference contents.

Persistent Chat Server requires a Back End Server role, and may include an additional role, **Compliance Back End**, to keep track of the messages published in Persistent Chat Server if required by local regulations or laws.

From the planning point of view, we need to keep the following points in mind:

- Some roles (such as archiving and monitoring) are always collocated on the Front End, while other roles (such as Mediation server) can be collocated depending on the scenario. Edge, and Director always require a dedicated server.

- Archiving, monitoring, and Persistent Chat require a database for each one. For this we could use a dedicated database or instance; collocate the databases on the SQL Express installation that is part of Front End, or collocate the databases on SQL Server that has the Back End role for an existing pool.

Enterprise Edition Front End, Mediation server, Director server, and Persistent Chat Server can be configured in a **pool** (that is, a group of servers having the same features installed). Pools are an important feature for high availability and load balancing (usually, the mechanism used is DNS load balancing, but hardware load balancing is supported as well).

The previously mentioned list does not include additional servers, such as Exchange and SharePoint. If these servers are present, they will be able to interact with Lync in a native manner to create an additional set of features.

Well-known examples of the integration include the presence of indicators in the Outlook client and Lync meeting integration with calendar (if Exchange is present), or any skill-based search that enables us to search for a person in Lync using the professional expertise recorded in SharePoint as criteria.

Installation steps and logic

The first necessary phase of a Lync 2013 deployment will be the planning phase, which includes a list of the features we make available, the availability and continuity requirements we have, the telephony and network configuration we need, and so on. Although design is not a topic we will explore in this book, it is something really important for a successful implementation of Lync in your company.

Talking about the design phase, the **Planning Tool** for Lync Server 2013 released at the end of February 2013 is really a good tool, with a wizard that asks for some basic information about the deployment, creates a base topology with suggestions on the required Lync roles and additional servers, and creates a list of the required system resources, a schema of the names and IPs of the deployment, and so on.

We are able to divide the deployment of Lync into three different phases:

- **Infrastructure setup**: This phase will have you perform the following steps:
    1. Join all the servers to the domain (excluding the Edge server that we will talk about in *Chapter 3, Deploying Lync Mobility and External Users Access*).
    2. Prepare the Active Directory.
    3. Set up the DNS.
    4. Configure the certificate infrastructure to use an **Internal Certificate Authority** (**Internal CA**).
    5. Install the required database infrastructure.

Lync 2013 supports high availability of Back End using **SQL mirroring**. SQL mirroring can be asynchronous (with no automated failover and failback) or synchronous (granting an automated response to failures). We will see the deployment of synchronous mirroring, using three servers.

    6. Check the routing and firewall rules (refer to *Ports and Protocols for Internal Servers* at http://technet.microsoft.com/en-us/library/gg398833.aspx).

- **Topology building**: The second phase is all about selecting the kind of deployment and topology that suit our needs, and implementing its parameters with Lync Topology Builder.
- **Lync installation**: The third phase installs Lync 2013 along with the services we had planned to install during the design of the topology in Topology Builder.

All we talked about is represented in the following diagram:

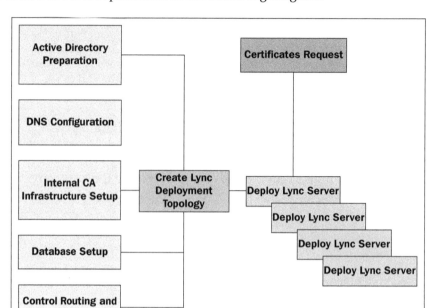

You would like to know

The deployment topology will be created using Topology Builder.

In the third phase, there are three required conditions to install any Lync feature or service:

- The server must be in the topology we designed using Topology Builder, and must match the FQDN we have used in the design of our topology

- The server needs access to the **Central Management Store** (**CMS**) database that contains all the configuration data of Lync (the Edge role, as we will see later, requires and exports the .zip file containing the CMS)

- The server has to know that the name of the topology is related to itself

A schema of our example environment

In this section we will see all the configuration steps required to deploy a working Lync environment. The additional configuration required for external user access will be explained in *Chapter 3, Deploying Lync Mobility and External Users Access*.

The final result will be like the one shown in the following diagram:

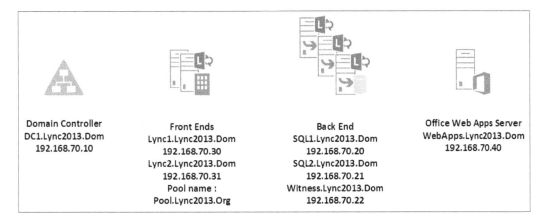

We have the base information in the following table:

Name	Role	IP
dc1.lync2013.dom	domain controller	192.168.70.10
lync1.lync2013.dom	lync front end	192.168.70.30
lync2.lync2013.dom	lync front end	192.168.70.31
pool.lync2013.org	lync pool name	192.168.70.30
pool.lync2013.org	lync pool name	192.168.70.31
sql1.lync2013.org	sql server – lync back end	192.168.70.20
sql2.lync2013.org	sql server – lync back end	192.168.70.21
witness.lync2013.org	sql server - witness	192.168.70.22
webapps.lync2013.dom	office web apps server	192.168.70.40

As we can see, we have used two different domains (this is a "typical" situation):

- The Active Directory domain name (available only to the internal network), lync2013.dom, to which we have joined our servers

- The public name of our SIP domain (in this example, Lync2013.org), which we will use to give access to external users

Infrastructure setup

The four steps of this phase (preparing the Active Directory, modifying the DNS, configuring Internal CA, and deploying the SQL database) can be executed in any order because no one is a prerequisite to the other.

At the moment we are going to configure only the internal services; therefore, the firewall configuration should not be an issue.

We need to extend the Active Directory schema with classes and attributes that are required by Lync Server.

For the previously mentioned operation, our forest and domain have to be at least Windows Server 2003 native level (that is why all domain controllers must have at least the Windows Server 2003 operating system).

 A list of supported Active Directory topologies is available here at *Active Directory Support* (http://technet.microsoft.com/en-us/library/gg425756.aspx).

There are three different ways to extend the schema:

- Using the Lync Server Deployment Wizard
- Using the Lync Server Management Shell
- Using ldifde.exe

In text we will follow the most common approach. To streamline the installation process, we will use the deployment wizard on the first Front End Server that we are going to deploy. If we want to use a different method, we can start by referring to *Preparing Active Directory Domain Services* at http://technet.microsoft.com/en-us/library/gg398607.aspx.

 The same thing is effective for Topology Builder, so usually it is used on the first server.

The second part of setting up the infrastructure requires you to manually add Lync records to the internal DNS.

Deploying certificates and DNS

The recent application of a change to the Baseline Requirements for the Issuance and Management of Publicly-Trusted Certificates (http://www.digicert.com/internal-names.htm) implies that it will not be possible in a few years to use internal names in our certificates, so a split-brain DNS configuration (with the public zone published on the internal DNS and the public FQDN related to internal addresses) or pinpointing DNS are the suggested solutions.

Usually, we will deploy two kinds of certificates:

- Certificates from our Internal CA for the internal services and connections
- Third-party certificates for the Internet-facing server, such as a reverse proxy and Edge

The first set of records that we need to add is the one related to the Lync Enterprise Front End pool.

As we said before, the pool can be balanced using DNS load balancing or a hardware load balancer.

The previous choice is *not* available for Lync's web services; therefore, if we also need to have web services in HA, we have to select a dedicated solution, such as a hardware load balancer paired with the DNS load balancing.

What we just said implies that there are different possible scenarios from a name-resolving point of view. A good part of them is addressed in the document *DNS Requirements for Front End Pools* at `http://technet.microsoft.com/en-us/library/gg412910.aspx`.

In our example, we will only have DNS load balancing with a couple of Lync Front End Servers, `Lync1` (192.168.70.30) and `Lync2` (192.168.70.31). The name of the pool will be `Pool`. The public domain will be `Lync2013.Org`.

Our DNS configuration will use the commonly used approach, "split-brain" DNS or "split" DNS, where we create an internal copy of the public DNS zone, replacing the IP addresses for Lync with the internal DNS records.

A drawback of the previously mentioned solution is that we will have to manage two "public" zones, the split-brain one and the zone published to the Internet.

An alternative could be to use a "pinpoint" DNS zone (refer to *Determine DNS Requirements* at `http://technet.microsoft.com/en-us/library/gg398758.aspx`), where we need to insert just the DNS records that will be different from the external zone, and point them to the internal network addresses. The rest of the DNS zone remain unchanged, and is referenced from the external, real master.

We need to perform the following steps to create a split-brain DNS:

1. Create a new zone in our internal DNS (the same where the domain zone is hosted, as shown in our example):

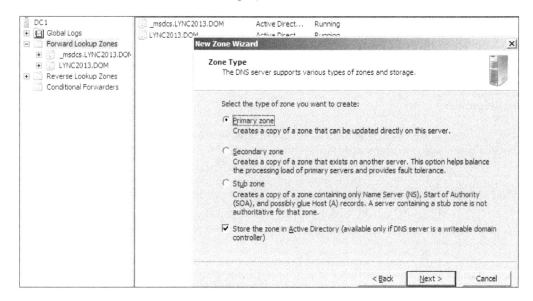

2. Name the zone as our public SIP domain `lync2013.org` (so that we have the "split-brain"), as shown in the following screenshot.

3. Add the A records for the Enterprise pool pointing to the IPs of each of the Front End Server units.

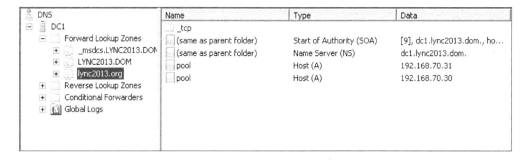

Now, we have to address another aspect: the DNS records for the web services.

Before we insert the information in the zone, we have to take an important decision regarding the URLs that we will expose to the external users.

Web services of Lync are tied to three different URLs: "**meet**", "**dial-in**", and "**admin**".

- Meet is the base URL for the meeting invitations we send, for example, to people outside our company or to someone who has no Lync client installed on his/her machine (and will participate using the Web App).

  A URI for a Lync meeting is similar to `https://meet.lync2013.org/fabrizio.volpe/Y6JTZ98S`.

  Launching it, a user with a Lync client installed locally will see the meeting start in the client, while a user without a client will have to access the meeting via the web interface of Lync.

- Dial-in is a record used to give users who will take part in a meeting using a telephone (for example, a traditional PSTN line), an interface where they can manage parameters such as a personal PIN and so on.

- Admin is used to publish the administrative console of Lync.

The only record really needed in Lync is meet, while dial-in is interesting only if we will use Enterprise Voice with dial-in conferencing and admin is something that we have to evaluate for every different deployment.

As we read in the document *Planning for Simple URLs* at `http://technet.microsoft.com/en-us/library/gg398287.aspx`, there are various options available.

I prefer to use a common "root" in the URI, because acting this way, we may need a single name in the certificate (let's say `meet`).

In our test deployment, we will have `meet` as the common path, and so we will need only two additional A records pointing `meet` to the Front End Servers that are added, as we can see in the following screenshot:

| meet | Host (A) | 192.168.70.30 |
| meet | Host (A) | 192.168.70.31 |

As we said before, the web services have high availability only if paired with a hardware load balancer. So, the configuration we have seen right now will use round robin to work (that is, in case of a failure, 50 percent of users trying to launch a Lync meeting from the internal network will experience failure).

Automatic client sign-in

Depending on the version we are using (Lync 2013, Lync 2010, or Store app), the client will query the DNS for a list of specific records, and as soon as one of them is resolved, the client will use it for authentication.

The following schema should make things clear:

Client	Queried SRV records' order
Lync 2013	`lyncdiscoverinternal.<domain>,` `lyncdiscover.<domain>, _sipinternal._` `tcp.<domain>, _sip._tls.<domain>, sip.<domain>,` `sipexternal.<domain>`
Lync 2010	`_sipinternal._tcp.<domain>, _sip._tls.<domain>,` `sip.<domain>, sipexternal.<domain>`
Store app and client for mobile devices	`lyncdiscoverinternal.<domain>,` `lyncdiscover.<domain>`

So, we have to add `lyncdiscoverinternal`, `_sipinternaltls._tcp`, and `sip`.

 Cumulative updates to desktop clients change the DNS location process from Lync Server 2010 (`http://technet.microsoft.com/en-us/library/gg398758.aspx`)

The SIP record will be pointed to the public IP of the Lync Edge server. This is because the configuration, using which we are going to test Lync Edge, will use the internal DNS as its primary DNS (an alternative is to use the hosts file on the server).

While `lyncdiscoverinternal` requires two A records with the IPs of the two Front End Servers and SIP via a simple A record to create the SRV record for `sipinternaltls._tcp`, we need to operate it as shown in the following screenshot, launching **Other New Records** from the DNS manager, and then selecting **Service Location SRV** (as depicted in *Required DNS Records for Automatic Client Sign-In* at `http://technet.microsoft.com/en-us/library/bb663700(v=office.12).aspx`).

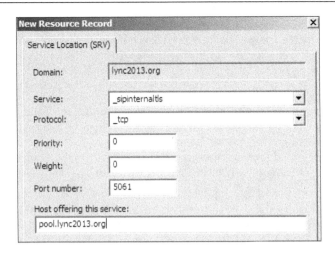

The final situation of the DNS zone that we have to create will look like the following screenshot:

_tcp			
(same as parent folder)	Start of Authority (SOA)	[9], dc1.lync2013.dom., ho...	static
(same as parent folder)	Name Server (NS)	dc1.lync2013.dom.	static
pool	Host (A)	192.168.70.31	static
pool	Host (A)	192.168.70.30	static
meet	Host (A)	192.168.70.30	
meet	Host (A)	192.168.70.31	
lyncdiscoverinternal	Host (A)	192.168.70.30	
lyncdiscoverinternal	Host (A)	192.168.70.31	

The configuration of the certification authority infrastructure is mandatory if our deployment will be based on certificates issued from an Enterprise CA.

The previously mentioned decision implies the limits for our Lync services when we will proceed to allow access to external users. Only clients and servers that accept our Internal CA as a trusted authority will be able to access our services, and that means our typical user will probably be one of our company workers or someone from a trusted partner network. The impact of the "internal" certificate is reduced if all the clients are part of our domain (because they will accept our Internal CA by default).

The other option (using a well-known public certification authority) is for sure easier to manage, but requires money because what we need for Lync is a costly **Unified Communication (UC)** certificate with multiple **Subject Alternative Names (SANs)**.

> There is no "easy way" or shortcut to bypass the need for certificates. Wildcard certificates (less costly) are not supported for the Edge services (they are usable only for the reverse proxy external interface). Also, using no certificate is not an option, because Lync has a high level of integrated security, and the server services (on the Edge or Front End) will simply not start with a wrong / not accepted certificate.

A detailed description of the deployment of an Enterprise CA is not included here, although a good starting point to understand it is the *Active Directory Certificate Services Step-by-Step Guide* article at http://technet.microsoft.com/en-us/library/cc772393(v=ws.10).aspx.

Now, talking about setting up the database, Lync Back End is a SQL deployment (more or less complex) without any Lync component or feature installed, but dedicated to host the Lync Central Management store.

The SQL Server deployment must be completed before creating and publishing the Lync topology by using Topology Builder.

The supported databases (only the 64-bit edition) are: SQL Server 2008 R2 Enterprise, SQL Server 2008 R2 Standard, SQL Server 2012 Enterprise, and SQL Server 2012 Standard.

> If we want to use database mirroring for Lync Back End, SQL 2008 R2 Standard Edition is not a valid choice.
>
> Lync Server 2013 Standard Edition automatically installs Microsoft SQL Server 2012 Express (64-bit edition) on each Lync server where the configuration store is required.

Some suggestions related to the installation of SQL for Lync are as follows:

- The features I will use in the example deployment are the ones we can see in the following screenshot:

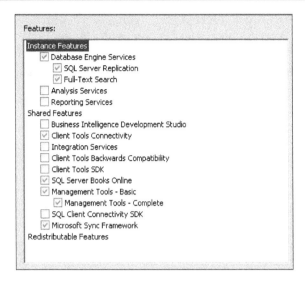

- Create a named instance for every Lync feature that requires a database to work (Archiving, Monitoring, and so on).

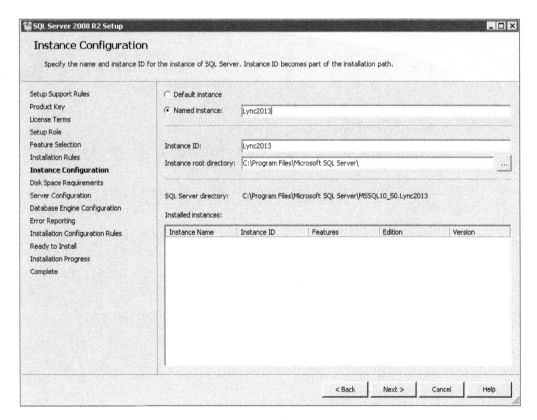

- Database mirroring is the best high availability feature you have for the Back End Servers of Lync. The first server (principle) will send the active transaction log record to the second (mirrored) server. The mirrored server applies the transaction log record one by one in sequence.

- Databases that work in mirroring need to be in "Full Recovery" mode, so watch out for the growth of the database logs.

- Mirroring requires two SQL servers and an optional third one (which can also be Express Edition) to act as a *Witness* that is required, so that the failover/failback of the principal database is automated.

Later, the Lync Topology Builder will require a file share during the process of creating mirror databases. We can create the share right now, giving the permissions to the accounts of the SQL servers (for the deployment of SQL1, SQL2, and Witness) as stated in Tim Harrington's blog post *Adding a SQL Mirror to an Existing Lync Server 2013 Back-End* (`http://howdouc.blogspot.it/2012/08/adding-sql-mirror-to-existing-lync.html`).

Topology building

If we are launching Topology Builder, it implies that we have completed the following checklist:

- Selected the kind of deployment we will use for our internal Lync servers (Front End pool or Standard Edition Servers)

- Selected the kind of certificates we will use

- Selected the features we will deploy

- Selected the geographical aspect of our Lync infrastructure (see Lync sites in *Chapter 2, Understanding Front End Pool Pairing*)

- Selected the number of additional servers we need considering the following list:

  - Edge
  - Reverse proxy
  - Mediation
  - Director

Often, it is the starting point that every company customizes with its parameters (especially from a naming and addressing point of view).

The required system resources are the same that we find in the TechNet documentation. The suggested system could be oversized for a small environment, so we have to adapt the design to our specific situation.

The preceding list is only to say that launching Topology Builder is the closing act of the design part.

After that, all we need to do is simply install Lync on the required servers, and make the whole mechanism work.

Of course, changes to an existing topology are possible, and in some cases are not difficult to make. However, some modifications (changing server or pool names, changing the deployment from Standard Edition to Enterprise Edition and the opposite way, and so on) are painful (requiring new certificates from an external authority) or impossible.

In the text, I suggest a staged approach to learn the meaning of the different steps. So we will deploy the internal servers, test them in depth, and then add the Edge and the other Internet-connected features (and test them too, obviously).

Creating all the topology in a single phase is a common way to reach the same result, and this is probably the action we will select when we are a bit more experienced.

In the following paragraphs, we will see a step-by-step installation of a Lync 2013 Enterprise Edition Front End with a SQL Back End enabled to mirroring. An Office Web Apps server will also be deployed (we will not look at the details related to this setup).

The Edge server and the reverse proxy will be added in *Chapter 3, Deploying Lync Mobility and External Users Access*.

The Lync installation

To understand the installation process in text, we will have it divided into three phases:

- Installation of Core Components
- Active Directory Preparation
- Lync Deployment

The first phase – preparing Windows 2012 for Lync 2013 and installing core components

A complete list of the required features and software to install Lync 2013 on Windows 2012 named *System Requirements for Servers Running Lync Server 2013* can be found at http://technet.microsoft.com/en-us/library/gg398588.aspx. A faster and lesser error-prone way to add the requirements is to use a PowerShell script. I have used a good one from Pat Richard's blog (http://www.ehloworld.com/1697).

 The script needs to know the path to your Server 2012 installation media. The script defaults to D: but can be configured for other locations.

We can add Silverlight right now, or it will be automatically installed the first time we launch the Lync Server Control Panel.

After the preparation (including the infrastructure steps and the system requirements installation), we are able to install Lync on the first Front End Server using the following steps:

1. Launch Setup.exe from Lync Installation Support"\Setup\amd64. This will be required for the installation of C++ 2012.

2. The setup process will require an installation path for Lync 2013.

3. The usual License Agreement request will appear, which will require you to select the **I accept the terms in the license agreement** checkbox.

   The installation of the core components will go on.

The Lync Server 2013 Deployment Wizard will appear on the screen as follows:

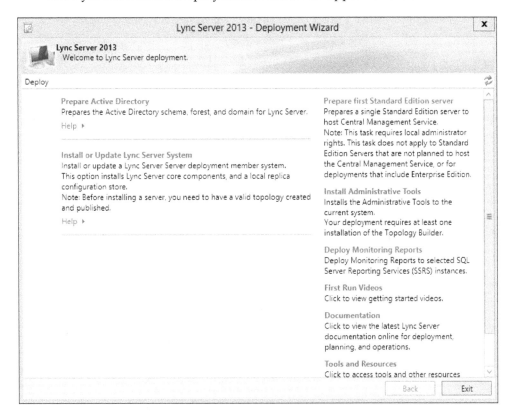

4. At this point, even the Lync Server Management Shell is installed on the server.

 Please remember that the deployment wizard is not used only during the first installation, but every time we add a role or component in the future.

The second phase – preparing the Active Directory

As a requirement to install Lync on our organization, we have to perform the following steps:

- Preparing the schema
- Preparing the forest
- Preparing the domain

The previously mentioned steps require accounts that have the rights to modify the Active Directory schema, forest, and domain, as stated in the *Preparing Active Directory Domain Services* article at `http://technet.microsoft.com/en-us/library/gg398607.aspx`.

From the deployment wizard, we will launch `Prepare Active Directory` and a menu with seven steps will be available:

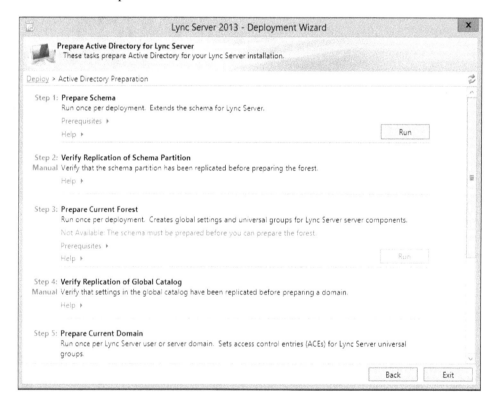

The first step will be **Prepare Schema**, the third will be **Prepare Current Forest**, and the fifth will be **Prepare Current Domain**.

All the other actions are dedicated to check the operation's result, and (in the last step) the addition of users in the group of Lync administrators, CSAdministrator.

The **Prepare Schema** screen will warn the user that the preparation of the schema is a "run once" operation. The operation will run, giving us "onscreen" updates on the various passages. When the step is completed, we can examine the log to check for (eventual) errors.

Prepare Current Forest and **Prepare Current Domain** are really similar to the schema preparation step.

The third phase – Lync deployment

Now, before going on with Topology Builder, we should have our SQL servers installed, a clear idea of our network from the connectivity point of view, and a plan for the names of the internal services too.

A reliable file share is also required (and usually it is suggested to use a file server cluster). The share will contain information that is accessed from all the servers and are store in three folders. The Lync File Share is used to house a bunch of Lync Shared Resources between servers. Once up and running, the server generates three subfolders: 1-ApplicationServer-1, 1-CentralMgmt-1, and 1-Webservices-1.

In our deployment, the share will be hosted on the Witness server of the SQL mirroring.

 Your mirror database instance must provide the same permissions and roles that are granted to your principal database instance.

During the design of the topology, we will be required to also insert the name of the Office Web Apps server. The installation of this server can be done before we launch Topology Builder or after (in the second scenario we will create a "pointer" to the server).

The steps to complete the Web Apps server installation are the ones you can read, for example, in Doug Deitterick's blog (http://blogs.technet.com/b/dodeitte/archive/2012/09/10/office-web-apps-server-amp-lync-server-2013.aspx).

Preparing and publishing the Lync topology

Use the following steps to prepare and publish the Lync topology:

1. To make Topology Builder available, we have to launch the deployment wizard and select **Install Administrative Tools**.

2. At the end of the process, the builder will be available in the Start menu of the server.

3. We have to select **New Topology** in the first screen and then configure the SIP domain as we can see in the following screenshot:

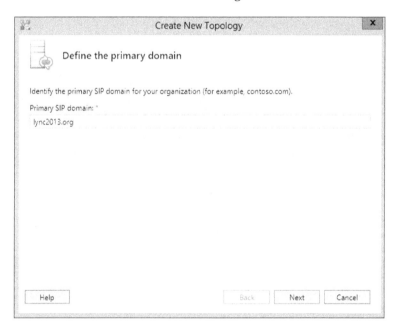

4. We will select no additional SIP domain and move to the **Define The First Site** menu. The information on sites we will insert in the wizard, especially if we have a single site, are not critical.

5. At the end of the previous procedure, we will have a wizard to deploy the Lync Front End as we can see in the following screenshot:

6. As foresighted, we will deploy an Enterprise Front End pool. The name of the pool will be `pool.lync2013.org`, and we will use the public FQDN and a split-brain / pinpoint DNS to resolve the name from the internal network, as explained earlier in the chapter:

7. We will add the two Front End Servers to the pool using their Active Directory / internal domain FQDN as shown in the following screenshot:

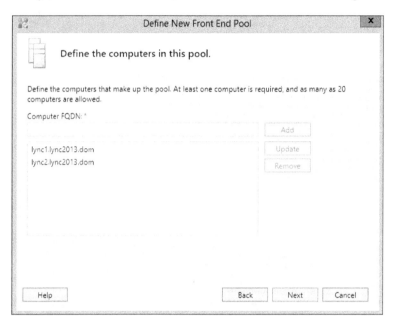

8. Now, we will add the **Conferencing** feature as we can see in the forthcoming screenshot:

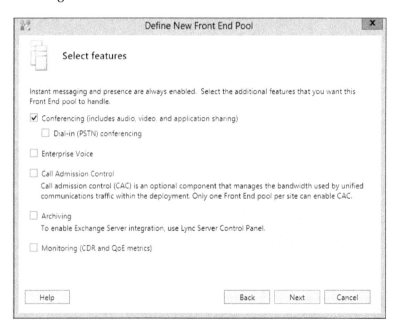

Enterprise Voice and Call Admission Control will be explained in *Chapter 3, Deploying Lync Mobility and External Users Access* and *Chapter 4, Introducing the Lync Mediation Server*. Dial-in conferencing is used to enable users with a telephonic connection to take part in a Lync conference (if we have Enterprise Voice already deployed). Archiving and Monitoring have been described earlier.

9. We will not collocate a Mediation server or add the Edge server (for the moment). So we will go on simply selecting **Next**.

10. The configuration of the SQL Back End with mirroring will require some additional information (simply adding the three SQL servers we have planned as primary, mirror, and Witness, with the New button):

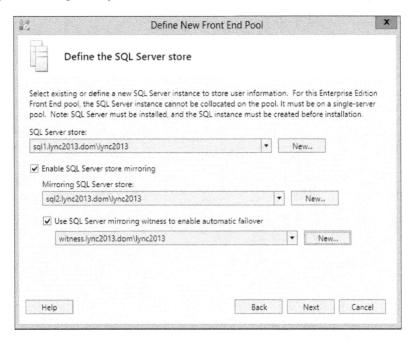

11. The path to the network share (FQDN `witness.lync2013.dom`, the file share, `LyncShare`) will be required:

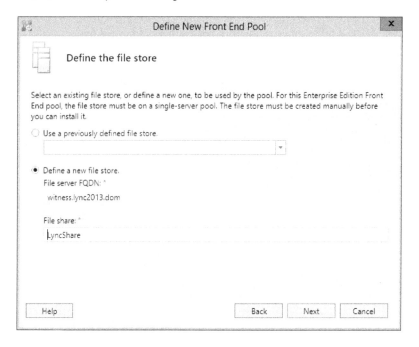

12. Enabling conferencing means that we will be asked for an Office Web Apps server (`webapps.lync2013.dom`), as we can see in the following screenshot:

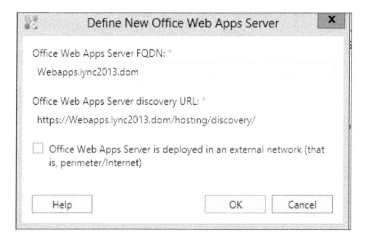

The screen will now show the association with the server we have defined at step 12.

13. Now, to make it easier to access the web services (and to spare some SAN names in the certificates), We will modify the "simple URLs" of Lync. That's an operation to run on the "root" of the topology by launching **Edit Properties**:

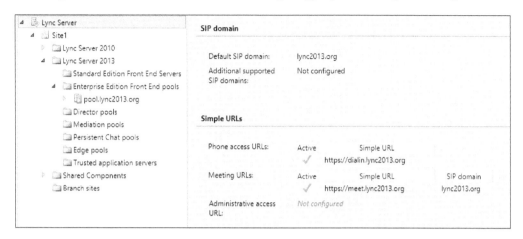

14. We have edited the URLs so that they have a common base name (`https://meet.lync2013.org`) and each service with its own path (`/dialin`, `/meet`, and `/admin`), as we can see in the following screenshot:

15. Now, it is time to publish the topology (the operation is launched from the Lync Server root in the topology view), as in the following screenshot:

16. After the first screen, we will be asked for the location of the Central Management server (in our example, it will be the pool itself). Usually, we would prefer to click on **Advanced...** and select **Use SQL Server instance defaults** (the modification is shown in the following two screenshots):

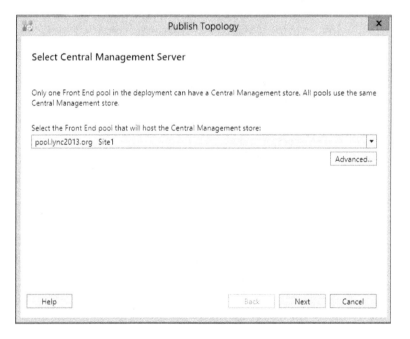

We are able to modify the path where database files and logs will be placed. If we have no special requirements, the default selection is a good solution.

⦿ Use SQL Server instance defaults
This option will place the database and log files based on target SQL Server instance settings. If you choose this option, read the product documentation on how to determine the best paths for optimal performance and use SQL Manager to change the paths appropriately

17. Next is the creation of the database (again, I suggest that you click on the **Advanced...** menu to select **Use SQL Server instance defaults**).

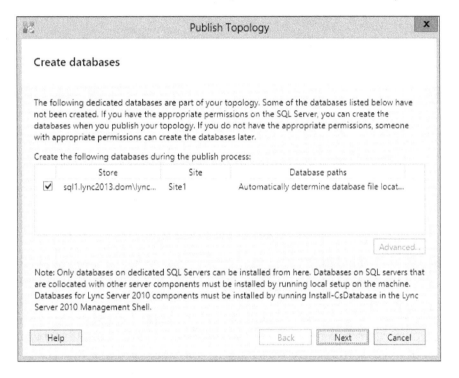

18. To create the mirrored database, we will be asked for a share. We will use the share previously created on the Witness server, as shown in the following screenshot. We could prefer to create a new share to split the Lync and database traffic.

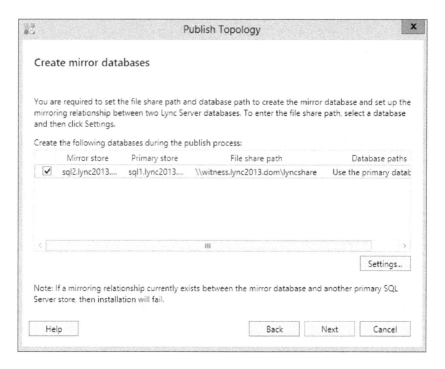

19. At the end of the process, we should see a screen containing a summary of the operations result, the access to the log, and a checklist of steps still waiting to be completed.

20. SQL primary and mirror should be in a synchronized/restoring state (we can verify that from SQL Server Management Studio), and the share should be populated with folders and data (we are able to check this by opening the folder).

Installing Lync Server components

The following steps will now help you to install the components associated with Lync Server:

1. Now, going back to the Lync Server deployment wizard, we can launch **Install or Update Lync Server System**.

Install or Update Lync Server System
Install or update a Lync Server Server deployment member system.
This option installs Lync Server core components, and a local replica
configuration store.
Note: Before installing a server, you need to have a valid topology created
and published.

Help ▶

2. The first option, **Step 1: Install Local Configuration Store**, is required only once for every Lync Server.

3. The **Step 2: Setup Or Remove Lync Server Components** option will be required every time we add or remove a component or role from the server deployment (as shown in the following screenshot):

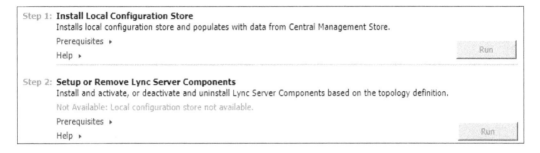

Step 1: **Install Local Configuration Store**
Installs local configuration store and populates with data from Central Management Store.
Prerequisites ▶
Help ▶   Run

Step 2: **Setup or Remove Lync Server Components**
Install and activate, or deactivate and uninstall Lync Server Components based on the topology definition.
Not Available: Local configuration store not available.
Prerequisites ▶
Help ▶   Run

4. For these steps, we simply need to hit the **Run** button and accept the default settings. When we set up or remove a component, the server will check its FQDN. If it matches the topology, the configuration will go on.

5. As usual, the result of the step will be shown in the ending screen with an available access to the logs for details.

Installing and assigning certificates

Now, we will have a look at the following steps to install and assign certificates:

1. **Step 3: Request, Install or Assign Certificates** allows us to create certificate requests, obtain the certificate directly (if we use an Enterprise CA), and apply them to Lync.

2. We can go with the **Request** button to forward our certificate's request to our enterprise CA:

3. After a starting screen that simply requires **Next**, we are able to select and send the request immediately (that's our situation) or prepare only the request (typically choose **Send the request immediately to an online certification authority**):

4. We have to select our CA and then **Next**:

5. If we do not need to add alternate credentials or specify an alternate template, we can simply hit **Next** in the two screenshots that follow.

   The screen that you will see in the following screenshot is important, not because we can select a friendly name for the certificate, but because we have to specify that the private key must be exportable (selecting the flag button).

A certificate with a private key that is not exportable is not good for our needs (in our example, we will export it from this server to the other Front End and this does not work without this option enabled):

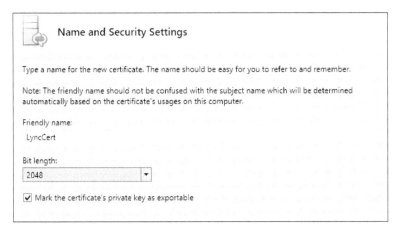

6. Organization information (shown in the following two screenshots) is critical only if we are going to communicate with an external CA that may require a verification of our company data. The following screenshot shows the screen that displays a list of names that will be in the certificate:

7. We have to select the flag related to our SIP domain to add the names required for automatic sign-in and other features:

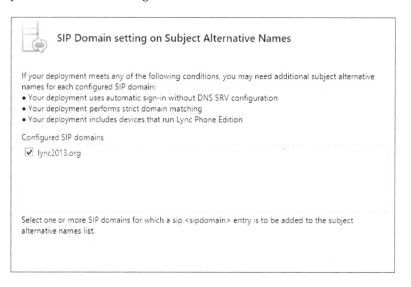

8. In **Configure Additional Subject Alternative Names**, we can add the name of the second Front End (Lync2.lync2013.dom), so that we can use the same certificate on both nodes (this is not mandatory, of course).The request process will run and contact our Enterprise CA.

9. When the certificate is ready, we can assign it automatically, leaving the flag selected:

Lync 2013 requires an OAuth certificate for server-to-server authentication that is required to talk with Exchange 2013 and SharePoint 2013 (this is really important if we want to integrate with Exchange UM). There are a lot of good blogs on this topic, such as this one at `http://social.technet.microsoft.com/wiki/contents/articles/13168.integrating-exchange-2013-owa-and-lync-server-2013.aspx` from Fernando Lugão Veltem. We can assign the certificate with the **Assign** button from the same screen where we create the requests.

10. If everything is well configured, using **Step 4: Start Services** we can check the server to see if Lync-related services are starting as expected.

11. Now we can verify server logs, the Windows event logs, and test Lync Server 2013 from a client. It is also a good point to install the latest updates and patches for our Lync Server.

 Sometimes, we could have the Lync services hung in the starting phase for a long time. A good starting point to troubleshoot the cause of this error could be at this site `http://www.bullspit.co.uk/2013/01/05/lync-2013-front-end-server-starting/`.

The deployment steps are to be repeated on the second Front End (`Lync2.lync2013.dom`).

Public certificates on the Lync Front End

In *Chapter 3, Deploying Lync Mobility and External Users Access*, we will acquire SSL certificates from a third-party CA for our Edge and reverse proxy. We will have to apply the aforementioned certificate on the Front End servers as well (at least for the web services dedicated to the external users).

We can work on it using the same administrative interface we have seen in step 3 in the previous section.

If we have required public certificates that also include the FQDN related to our internal domain, we can simply replace the certificate released from our internal CA. However, this solution that includes the FQDN that is not reachable from the Internet in a third-party certificate will not be available after November 1, 2015.

What we can do then is use the capability of Lync to use different certificates on the web services dedicated to the internal and to the external users (as you can see in the following screenshot).

So, we are able to apply the certificate from the internal CA on the internal web services interface and the certificate from the third-party CA (containing only the FQDN of our public domain) on the external web services interface.

Summary

This chapter has been an introduction to the basic concepts of Lync and the first deployment we need to perform (Lync Front End).

The next chapter will focus on a new feature of Lync 2013 dedicated to continuity: Front End pairing.

2
Understanding Front End Pool Pairing

In this chapter we will talk about Front End pool pairing, a new form of continuity introduced by Lync 2013. This solution is really important in order to go beyond a few limits that were present in previous solutions for high availability and disaster recovery. The aforementioned are critical aspects of a Lync deployment, especially if we are offering Enterprise Voice services.

In Lync 2010, we had high availability with Enterprise pools (so that it was possible to have up to 10 Front End Servers tied together), and a clustered SQL database as **Lync Back End**. In the preceding scenario, often a weak point was the SQL 2008 cluster, which is clearly a bottleneck from a continuity point of view, requiring a shared storage and posing a heavy limit to geographically dispersed solutions.

A basic form of disaster recovery was named **Backup Registrar,** and was based on the "pairing" of one or more Enterprise Edition pools / Standard Edition servers with another Enterprise pool / Standard Edition server installed on a different Lync site. The features made available to a user homed on a failed pool (or a Standard Edition server) were limited to Enterprise Voice (not all the services were available anyway), and a limited subset of other services, such as intra-site instant messaging (IM) and audio/video (A/V).

The aforementioned settings require an introduction to the concept of a site. In Lync, a site is a logical object created through the Topology Builder. We may consider a Lync site as a set of Lync servers linked with a high-speed data connection (LAN or campus with a fiber optic connection) and low latency (with a maximum around 150 milliseconds end to end). Please remember that there is no direct association with other logical objects used by other Microsoft software that have the same name, such as the sites used by Active Directory.

Introduction to Front End pairing

The whole mechanism is based on the approach that Lync 2013 uses to manage the "presence" database (each Front End Server now controls the presence database) and on the **Windows Fabric** component, which is used to keep user data in sync on all the Front End servers. We will cover the Windows Fabric component later in this chapter.

When a pool hosting the **Central Management Store** (**CMS**) is paired with another pool, it creates a backup of the CMS and a Master/Standby relationship between the two database instances.

The aforementioned mechanism explains why, in Lync 2013, the dependency on the Back End Server has been "relaxed" (what happens is named **lazy writes** — the SQL Server database is updated mainly for the eventuality of a disaster recovery). To manage the new logic of the presence database, the algorithm used in Lync 2010 to determine where a user was homed (also if a failure occurred on one or more Front Ends) has been changed.

Now, we have Lync 2013 automatically creating the so-called **user groups** (a whole new concept), and distributing the users inside the aforementioned groups. An algorithm is used to select the server where users are homed and the membership in the groups. Each one of the user groups is tied to a primary, secondary, and tertiary Front End Server.

 The aforementioned logic based on a minimum of three Front End Servers is the reason why it is recommended to deploy a minimum of three servers in an Enterprise pool.

Deployment with a reduced number of Front End Servers is supported, and we will see only the primary Front End Server, or primary and secondary Front End Servers, for the user groups.

With a configuration such as the one we have just explained, in case of a Front End Server outage, the user groups that have that server as primary will fail over to the secondary server.

If the secondary is not available or fails (and the primary is still not working), the groups will fail over to the tertiary server. Any additional failover will require the election of another Front End, and the creation of a new user group for the users.

In the following screenshot, we see the failover process when two Front End Servers become unavailable:

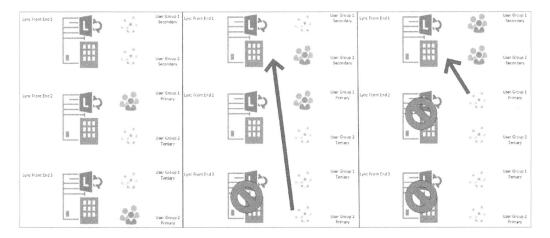

- Users with a primary group on Front End 3 fail on their secondary group on Front End 1 as soon as Front End 3 is no longer available
- When Front End 2 becomes unavailable too, the users with a primary group located there will also fail to Front End 1

If we add more servers to the pool, the groups will be rebalanced to distribute the load on more nodes.

 If we need to know the user group assignment in a 2013 pool, we can use the `Get-csuserpoolinfo -identity "user"` cmdlet.

Such mechanisms require that we have an underlying service to replicate data between Front End Servers and maintaining up to three copies of the user data on the Front End Servers. **Windows Fabric** is a service installed during the server setup of Lync Server 2013, and is the technology on which we base the aforementioned synchronization.

The result of moving a part of the data from SQL to the Front End Servers is that we are able to maintain presence and contacts during a Back End service interruption.

Associating Lync pools

Before we see the steps required to configure the association between Lync pools, we need to know some limits that we have to respect in order to keep a "supported" situation.

The document on which we have to base our deployment is *Best Practices for Pairing Front End Pools* at `http://technet.microsoft.com/en-us/library/jj204697.aspx`. The following list includes all the most important constraints:

- **Enterprise Edition pools** can be paired only with other Enterprise Edition pools. Similarly, Standard Edition pools can be paired only with other Standard Edition pools.

  The Topology Builder will also allow us to pair pools that are not of the same kind, but this is not to be considered as a validation.

- **Physical pools** can be paired only with other physical pools. Similarly, virtual pools can be paired only with other virtual pools.

- Pool pairing is bidirectional; if a pool is associated to another pool, it is not possible to pair an additional pool (that is, there is no support for a three-pool pairing because the relation is 1:1).

- It is recommended to have the pools in different Lync sites located in two geographically separated locations with a really good network connection (10 Mb/s or faster) if we also need to have disaster recovery.

- Each pool should have enough resources to manage the workload in case of a fail from the paired pool (again, it is important especially for a disaster-recovery plan).

When we configure a Lync pool to be the backup registrar of another pool, the **Lync Server Backup Service** is installed. This service is used to keep user information and almost all the other data in sync between the associated pools.

Failover and failback options

When we start a failover or a failback operation, we have a period of time that is required for the process to actually complete. Both the actions are manually initiated and that implies that the time periods mentioned in the TechNet article, *Recovery Time for Pool Failover and Pool Failback*, at `http://technet.microsoft.com/en-us/library/jj205079.aspx`, are calculated from the moment the administrator actually launches the disaster procedure. The value indicated in the documentation as the recovery point objective (30 minutes) indicates that if we launch a failover or a failback, all the data changed in the 30 minutes between the time the failure procedure is accomplished (T) and 30 minutes before (T-30) could be lost.

As we will see, the administrator manually invokes the failover procedures using the Lync Server Management Shell. In the following schema, the various steps related to a failover and failback scenario are shown:

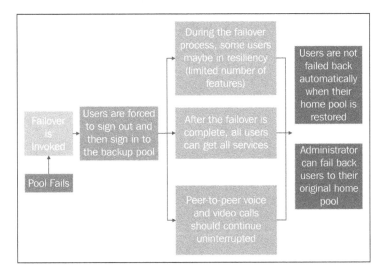

Managing server failures

I have prepared an environment to test the pool pairing failover and failback based on two different sites (Site 1 and Site 2) and a Standard Edition server in each site, as shown in the following diagram:

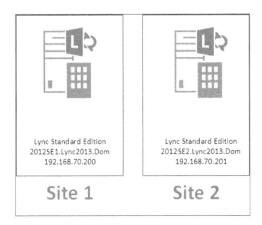

1. The first step is to modify the topology using the Topology Builder. We have to select one of the Standard Edition servers and select **Edit Properties**.

2. The modifications we have to perform in the Front End properties (as shown in the following screenshot) are as follows:

    1. Modify the **Resiliency** parameter.

    2. Check **Associated backup pool**.

    3. Select the other server from the drop-down menu.

    4. Check **Automatic failover and failback for Voice** (if we want to use such a feature).

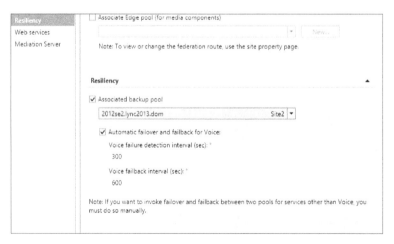

3. When we publish the topology, we will receive a to-do list to complete the configuration.

4. To activate the changes, we have to run the setup file or remove the Lync server components (in the Lync deployment) on both Lync Front Ends.

5. One of the things that will happen now is the installation of the Lync Backup Service, as shown in the following screenshot:

```
Installing MgmtServer.msi(Feature_MGMTServer, Feature_FTA, Feature_Master)...success
Installing BackupService.msi(Feature_LyncBackup)...success
```

6. To check the status of the pairing, we have to launch the Lync Management Shell and run the `Get-CsBackupServiceStatus` command, as follows:

```
PS C:\Users\administrator.LYNC2013> Get-CsBackupServiceStatus

cmdlet Get-CsBackupServiceStatus at command pipeline position 1
Supply values for the following parameters:
PoolFqdn: 2012se1.lync2013.dom

ActiveMachineFqdn    OverallExportStatus OverallImportStatus BackupModules
-----------------    ------------------- ------------------- -------------
2012SE1.Lync2013...        FinalState         NormalState (UserServices.Pr...


PS C:\Users\administrator.LYNC2013> _
```

7. If everything is working properly, we can test the failover with the `Invoke-CsManagementServerFailover –BackupSqlServerFQDN 2012SE2.Lync2013.Dom –BackupSQLInstanceName RTC –Force` command. The result is shown in the following screenshot:

```
Administrator: Lync Server Management Shell                          _ □ x
PS C:\Users\administrator.LYNC2013> Invoke-CsManagementServerFailover –BackupSql
ServerFQDN 2012SE2.Lync2013.Dom –BackupSQLInstanceName RTC –Force

Confirm
This cmdlet fails over Central Management Server to the pool that backs up the
current active Central Management Server.

  Current State:
    Central Management Server Pool: "2012SE1.Lync2013.dom"
    Central Management File Store: "\\2012SE1.Lync2013.dom\share"
    Central Management Store: "2012SE1.Lync2013.dom\rtc"
    Central Management Store SCP: "2012SE1.Lync2013.dom\rtc"

  Proposed State:
    Central Management Server Pool: "2012se2.lync2013.dom"
    Central Management File Store: "\\2012se2.lync2013.dom\share"
    Central Management Store: "2012se2.lync2013.dom\rtc"
    Central Management Store SCP: "2012se2.lync2013.dom\rtc"

Warning: The cmdlet is not being run from a computer in the pool
'2012se2.lync2013.dom', which is where the Central Management service will be
failed over. As a result the cmdlet will not be able to verify the status of
Lync Server Master Replicator Agent service and Lync Server File Transfer Agent
service in the target pool. Run the cmdlet from a computer in the pool
'2012se2.lync2013.dom' so that it can verify the service states.

Do you want to failover the Central Management Server, Central Management
store, and file store in the current topology and assign permissions for
computers in Active Directory? (Note: Please read the help provided for this
cmdlet using the Get-Help cmdlet before you proceed.)
[Y] Yes  [A] Yes to All  [N] No  [L] No to All  [S] Suspend  [?] Help
(default is "Y"):a
WARNING: The Central Management Server failover completed successfully but the
following additional steps may be required:

Check that Lync Server Master Replicator Agent service and Lync Server File
Transfer Agent service are running on the following computers. It may be
required to run local setup on these computers if the services are not
installed:
    - 2012se2.lync2013.dom

WARNING: "Invoke-CsManagementServerFailover" processing has completed with
warnings. "1" warnings were recorded during this run.
WARNING: Detailed results can be found at
"C:\Users\administrator.LYNC2013\AppData\Local\Temp\2\Invoke-CsManagementServer
Failover-2ebb1117-3a93-44e8-be25-762bc43a5be3.html".
```

During the failover and the subsequent failback procedure, we could receive some warnings. Usually they are informational ones; the logfiles generated during the process are the first tool to troubleshoot issues if they arise.

8. It is now possible to verify whether the users have been moved from one Standard Edition server to the other. The easiest way is to open the Lync Control Panel and look for the server where the users are now homed.

9. We are able to fail back the users with the `Invoke-CsPoolFailBack -PoolFqdn 2012SE2.Lync2013.Dom` command.

We could have errors in the process, and those can be resolved by following the articles at `http://social.technet.microsoft.com/Forums/nl-NL/lyncserverpreview/thread/95b6528f-7521-48c7-99e2-223bddeb7b0c` and `http://ocsguy.com/2012/11/06/lync-backup-service-related-cmdlets-fail/`. The first error, **Can not update database xds since the database state is not up to date**, seems to be a common one.

Summary

The Front End pairing feature is extremely important for the resiliency of our company's Lync deployment. During the tests, we examined the mechanisms and settings required for that feature.

In the next chapter, the focus will move to the external users and the steps we need to take to make our Lync environment available to them.

3
Deploying Lync Mobility and External Users Access

Mobility is one of the aspects of Lync 2013 that is constantly changing at a fast pace. The release of **Lync Server 2013 Cumulative Update 1 (CU1)** in February 2013 is a really important release, adding support to the Lync 2013 Mobile clients that released during March 2013 for Windows Phone, iPhone and iPad, and Android.

> For more information regarding the setup of CU1, please refer to *How to Apply Lync Server 2013 Cumulative Updates* at `http://blogs.technet.com/b/dodeitte/archive/2013/02/27/how-to-apply-lync-server-2013-cumulative-updates.aspx`.

The Lync 2013 versions of the client have support for voice and video over Wi-Fi and cellular data networks. Additional features, such as **Voice Mail access**, **Contacts list**, and **Lync call**, are also available.

The deployment of support for mobile devices implies the use of two additional servers (**the Edge role** and a **reverse proxy**) to the deployment of Lync we have seen in the *Infrastructure setup* section in *Chapter 1, Installing a Lync 2013 Enterprise Pool*.

The aforementioned requirements are also mandatory if we want to enable any kind of client to use our Lync deployment (or to use the Lync Web App) from the external networks.

Using the Lync Server 2013 planning tool (that we have introduced in the *Installation steps and logic* section in *Chapter 1, Installing a Lync 2013 Enterprise Pool*), the simplest configuration we can obtain is the one shown in the following diagram:

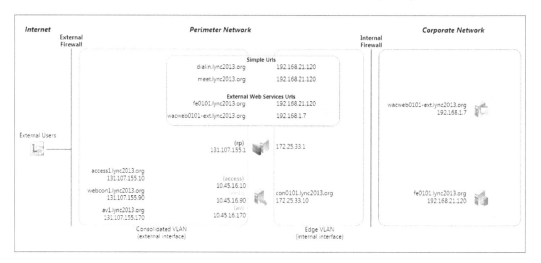

A lot to talk about there, so a good step would be to examine the design phase splitting it into four pieces:

- The DNS configuration
- The reverse proxy
- Front End modifications
- Edge

 Both Edge and the reverse proxy require at least an internal IP address and an external/public IP. For Edge, as we will see later, the most used deployment is the one with three public IPs.

The DNS configuration

To enable Lync mobile clients to connect without having to manually add the parameters of the Lync services (also known as **Autodiscover Sevices**), we have to create two different records, one on the internal DNS and one on the public DNS:

- `LyncDiscoverInternal`: This is an internal DNS CNAME (that is, an alias of another standard domain name) or a record to resolve the internal Autodiscover Service URL

- `LyncDiscover`: This is an external DNS CNAME or a record to resolve the external Autodiscover Service URL

The first record should point to our internal pool or Standard Edition server, while the second record, the "public" URL of Autodiscover, should be headed to the public address of the reverse proxy.

The reverse proxy

As mentioned earlier, the reverse proxy is required to make the web services of our Front End Server available to external users. The role of the reverse proxy is to publish resources to an external network, while creating a transparent and secure layer between the Internet user and our website and services. The connection will point to the records on the public DNS and so we will need rules to rewrite calls and direct them correctly to the internal servers.

Mobile clients make a heavy use of the web services of Lync, especially the Lync 2010 version that is basically an IM client (with push capabilities on some mobile devices).

The first decision we need to take here is about what kind of technology we are going to use for our reverse proxy.

A less costly solution could be the use of a reverse proxy on a Linux deployment or Internet Information Services (**IIS**) as in this post, *Using IIS ARR as a Reverse Proxy for Lync Server 2013* at `http://blogs.technet.com/b/nexthop/archive/2013/02/19/using-iis-arr-as-a-reverse-proxy-for-lync-server-2013.aspx`. If we need a more complete and secure solution, there is a really long list of vendors and products. You can refer to the TechNet page dedicated to certified load balancers for Lync at `http://technet.microsoft.com/en-us/lync/gg131938.aspx`.

> **Forefront Unified Access Gateway** (**UAG**) has well-known problems with Lync mobility, and is not a recommended solution. You can read more about this issue in the great post by *Ben Ari* titled *UAG, Lync Mobility and other Lync clients* (`http://blogs.technet.com/b/ben/archive/2012/11/09/uag-lync-mobility-and-other-lync-clients.aspx`).

Web services running on the Lync Front End

Depending on the form we have selected for the "simple URLs" used to publish Lync Front End web services (see the *Infrastructure setup* section in *Chapter 1*, *Installing a Lync 2013 Enterprise Pool*), the rewrite rules on the reverse proxy will change.

Lync installation creates rewrite rules inside the IIS site in the Front End Servers, so a little bit of testing is strongly advised. We have two sites (something we were able to see during the design of the Lync topology), an internal one and an external one (see the following screenshot):

The **external site** (that is, the one we will use to point to our reverse proxy) answers by default on two ports, 8080 and 4443. The internal website will be listening on the standard ports, 80 and 443. So, to summarize, we need to configure the rewrite rules so that users coming from the external network will call port 80 and 443 of the published server and be connected through the reverse proxy to the Lync Front End on port 8080 (if we plan to use HTTP) or 4443 (if we plan to use HTTPS).

Last but not least, if we are going to use HTTPS (which is the recommended solution) on the public interface of the reverse proxy, we have to apply an **SSL digital certificate** (these are small data files that digitally bind a cryptographic key to an organization's details, used to allow secure connections from a web server to a browser). The latter could be a wildcard certificate, because such a solution is supported for the simple URL. As a referral we can use the following TechNet article *Wildcard Certificate Support* (http://technet.microsoft.com/en-us/library/hh202161.aspx).

The decision is often related to the costs (that is, a wildcard certificate is really cheaper than a multiple SANs certificate).

A **Subject Alternative Names** (**SANs**) certificate allows for multiple domain names to be protected with a single SSL certificate.

Lync Edge

Lync Edge is the point where we make services such as Access Edge, A/V authentication, A/V Edge, Web Conferencing Edge, and XMPP proxy service available to the external users. We have the possibility to bind such services to three public addresses on the external interface of Edge, or to join them to three different ports joined to a single public IP. The decision between the configurations has an impact on costs and on the accessibility of the services.

The first solution requires three valuable public IPs dedicated to Edge, while the second one requires only one Internet address.

However, the latter design is more prone to difficulties that the access might face from the external networks because the ports that the external users will be required to open on Edge are out of the standard TCP/80 and TCP/443 that are allowed by almost all the enterprise proxies and firewalls.

Preparing Lync Edge

To deploy Lync Edge, we have to comply with the following requirements:

- Two network interfaces, configured as discussed earlier in the chapter.
- The server must be outside our domain.
- Lync Front End Servers and Lync Edge must be able to resolve each others' **Fully Qualified Domain Name (FQDN)**. Edge is usually located in a **Demilitarized Zone (DMZ)** network, so that we can:
    - Use one or more public DNS to resolve names from the "external" interface of Edge. We will have to add the FQDN of the Front End in the HOSTS file of Edge and vice versa.
    - Enable Edge to query our internal DNS and keep the same logic of split-brain (or pinpointing) we have seen in *Chapter 1, Installing a Lync 2013 Enterprise Pool*.

- We have to configure a DNS suffix for our Edge. This could be the name of our public zone (as shown in the following screenshot), and this is a good solution to keep compatibility with third-party certificates that should contain the Edge server name. The name has to match the one used in the Topology Builder.

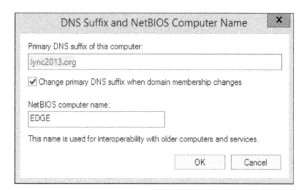

- If we plan to use certificates generated on the domain CA, we have to import the certificate of the root Certification Authority on the server.

Configuring Lync Edge

The steps for the configuration are as follows:

1. The first step of the configuration is to launch the Topology Builder, and we have to define the new Edge pool. After a welcome screen, we will be asked if we plan to deploy one or more Edge servers, as shown in the following screenshot:

2. The option to deploy a pool, as usual, is related to the need for high availability and continuity. The screenshot that follows will present the different options, and they are as follows:

   ° For Edge publishing (single IP or multiple IPs)

   ° For federation

   ° For XMPP federation

   Federation enables our Lync deployment to connect with other published Lync systems. The XMPP federation is used to communicate with services such as Google Talk.

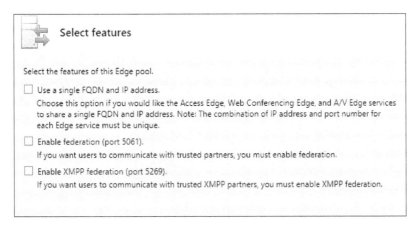

   If we choose to proceed with a single public address for all the services, both SIP and federation access will be listening on port 5061. In this chapter, I will assume that we are working with three public addresses for Edge.

3. We will receive a request to define which versions of IP we will use *and* (really important) if we are going to use NAT.

 Network Address Translation (NAT) is a mechanism used if we are running our Lync Edge behind a firewall. The real IPs of Edge are translated by the firewall to the ones people will see from the external network. Setup without NAT usually is related to a Lync Edge that is directly connected to the Internet with the network interfaces configured with public IPs.

4. The following screenshot will require the names of the external FQDN:

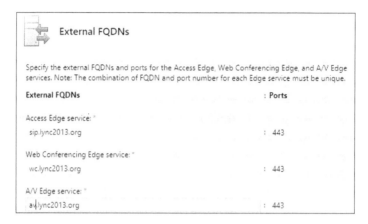

5. The next screen will require to define the internal IP address of the server; the value will be the network address of the network interface that will connect the server to the internal network (172.25.33.10 if we use the schema created with the Lync Server 2013 planning tool).

6. We will be asked to associate the public IPs of Edge with the different services (again, we will use the public addresses we have put in the planning tool):

 It is really important that the records we publish on the public DNS match the name, that is, the IP pairs we are setting during the aforementioned steps of the Topology Builder.

7. We will propose to associate Edge with one of our Front End Servers:

8. If we have one or more Mediation servers, we will be offered the opportunity to associate one or more with Edge.

This last step completes the preparation phase.

Copying the CMS on the Edge server

As usual, we will have to publish the topology, and then, before we go to set up the Lync components on Edge, we have an additional task to perform: exporting the CMS.

Edge is to be installed on a standalone server, so we have to export the CMS, copy the file on Edge, and then import the CMS.

1. We will launch an export command from a working Back End Server using Lync Management Shell:

   ```
   Export-CsConfiguration -File C:\temp\export.zip
   ```

2. Copy the compressed file on the Edge server.

3. Launch the deployment wizard on Edge. In the **Configure Local Replica of Central Management Store** page, we will select the **Import from a file** option.

The other steps are to be performed, as we have seen in *Chapter 1, Installing a Lync 2013 Enterprise Pool*, for the deployment of a Lync Front End.

Configuring for push notifications

The push notification is a cloud-based service used to send notifications to Lync mobile clients installed on devices such as Windows Phone, even if the application is inactive. The mechanism is used to notify the user of lost invitations to IM conversations or of waiting voice mail messages.

Lync 2013 mobile on Apple devices does not need push notification (required by the Lync 2010 mobile client).

An example of the process for push notification is explained in the *Understanding Push Notifications for Lync 2013 Mobility* article (`http://www.bhargavs.com/index.php/2013/03/28/configuring-lync-2013-mobility-for-push-notifications/`).

The configuration requires the following:

- To connect to Microsoft's hosted Lync platform, you will have to run the following command from the Lync Management Shell:

```
New-CsHostingProvider -Identity "LyncOnline" -Enabled $True
-ProxyFqdn "sipfed.online.lync.com" -VerificationLevel
UseSourceVerification
```

- To allow federation with Microsoft's push notification service, you will have to run the following command from the Lync Management Shell:

```
New-CsAllowedDomain -Identity "push.lync.com"
```

- To enable push notifications on the `site1` Lync site for Microsoft devices, you will have to run the following command from the Lync Management Shell:

```
Set-CsPushNotificationConfiguration -Identity
"site:site1" -EnableApplePushNotificationService $True
-EnableMicrosoftPushNotificationService -$True
```

- The following command is used to modify the federated users collection (the only allowed collection) of the configuration settings:

```
Set-CsAccessEdgeConfiguration -AllowFederatedUsers $True
```

Summary

During this chapter we have seen the required configurations and steps to make our Lync services available to the external users. The forthcoming chapter will be focused on a fundamental role for the Enterprise Voice: the Mediation server.

4
Introducing the Lync Mediation Server

After the previous chapter, dedicated to Lync mobility and external users access, we will introduce the Lync Mediation server that is part of every voice deployment, along with the dial plans, voice policies, and the voice routes that will be explained in *Chapter 5*, *Getting Started with Lync Enterprise Voice*.

Starting with Lync 2010, Microsoft has added some essential features regarding the enterprise voice, such as resiliency (users can continue making and receiving calls if the server, where they are homed becomes unavailable), call number manipulation (required to present the telephone numbers from Lync in a format that is compatible with the different hardware and telephonic providers), and media bypass (that is explained later in this chapter).

A big part of the "magic" is due to the Mediation server role of Lync. Mediation servers are responsible to manage the communication between the Front End Servers and the gateways, such as a SIP trunk or a PSTN gateway (see the *Mediation server Tasks* section). As we said in the *Lync Server Roles* section in *Chapter 1*, *Installing a Lync 2013 Enterprise Pool*, the role can be collocated on the Front End Servers (so its continuity is related to the Front End continuity), or it can be deployed as an autonomous single server or an autonomous pool (for continuity reasons).

 The only scenario that does *not* recommend collocating the Mediation server is a situation that includes an SIP trunk.

To clarify some of the concepts we will see in the chapter, we can use a modified version of the *Microsoft Lync Server 2013 Protocol Workloads Poster* from *Rui Maximo*.

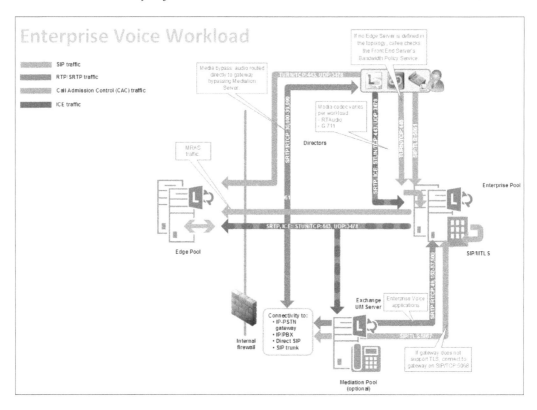

Configuring the Mediation server

Configuring a Mediation server takes place in the following two ways.

Configuring a collocated Mediation server

To configure a collocated Mediation server on an existing Lync Front End, we have to edit the properties of the aforementioned server and define the Mediation server parameters, as we can see in the following screenshot:

For a collocated Mediation server, we have to publish the new topology, and then run the **Setup or Remove Lync Server Components** from the **Lync Deployment Wizard**.

 TCP is used for gateways that do not support TLS. We might have to change either the gateway listening address or the Lync configuration because most gateways use TCP 5061.

Configuring a standalone Mediation server or a pool of Mediation servers

If we are creating a new pool or a single dedicated server, we have to operate in the Lync Topology Builder.

1. We have to define the server or pool name as shown in the following screenshot:

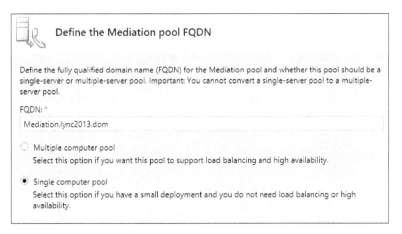

2. We are required to define the Front End that will be associated with the Mediation server as we can see in the following screenshot:

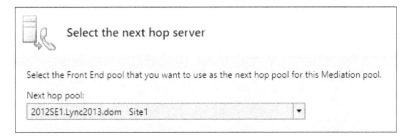

3. Another association we have to define is with the Lync Edge server, as it is suggested in the following screenshot:

4. This last step concludes the topology building phase. After we have published the topology, we will have to deploy the single server (or the servers in the pool) following the same steps we used for the Front End Servers in *Chapter 1, Installing a Lync 2013 Enterprise Pool*.

Mediation server tasks

The Mediation server performs the following operations:

- Identifying the type of network that a voice call will use
- Selecting the best codec for the aforementioned network
- Converting signals and media according to the previous points, such as translating SIP over TCP to SIP over TLS, translating media (G.711) on the gateway to RTAudio on CS, or for media traversal of NAT

 The most used codecs are: G711 (better quality but requires a network without packet loss) or RTAudio that is also able to work with a certain number of lost packets (RTAudio has a native error concealment module).

Talking about codecs, we should take a look at the document *Network Bandwidth Requirements for Media Traffic* (http://technet.microsoft.com/en-us/library/jj688118(v=ocs.15).aspx) that is really important for planning and understanding the bandwidth requirements for every single solution. If we are preparing a project we could also use the *Lync 2010 and 2013 Bandwidth Calculator* article at http://www.microsoft.com/en-us/download/details.aspx?id=19011.

Mediation server improvements in Lync 2013

In Lync 2013, we have some improvement features that were partially present in the 2010 version:

- **M:N trunk routing**: This is an evolution of the 1:N relation that enabled us to associate multiple gateways to a single Mediation server. Now we can associate the following:
    - ° A single Mediation server to multiple gateways
    - ° A single gateway to a single Mediation server with multiple trunks
    - ° A single gateway to multiple Mediation servers

- **Inter-trunk routing**: With this feature, Lync 2013 is enabled to act as a gateway between two or more different PBXs or to connect a PBX to a PSTN gateway.

- **Caller ID**: This is an option to translate the calling phone number from the E.164 format to the local dialing format (it may be required by the gateway).

- **Hybrid voice**: The on-premise deployment is now able to work with users hosted in the cloud on Office 365.

Media bypass

The Mediation server is able to decide if a client can be connected directly to a PSTN gateway (without traversing the server itself).

The preceding solution reduces latency; the number of points in which we could have packet loss or failures, saves WAN bandwidth and lowers the hardware requirements for the Mediation server (making it easier to collocate on the Front End).

It is also an essential feature for branch offices having a local PSTN gateway available, so that local clients are able to connect to the public switched line with no need to talk to the Mediation server (that could be located on a central site).

To deploy media bypass we have some requirements:

- The voice gateway, PBX, or ITSP on our network (defined as Mediation server peers) must support media bypass

- The Mediation server peers must accept media traffic directly from the Lync Server

- Lync clients and the Mediation server peer must be well connected (local network or high bandwidth geographical network)

There are two ways to configure media bypass:

- By selecting the **Always bypass** option in the global settings
    - ° The entire network is considered as a single site
    - ° No call admission control

    The aforementioned configuration will be applied from the **Lync Control Panel | Network Configuration** tab.

    The properties we are able to edit are shown in the following screenshot:

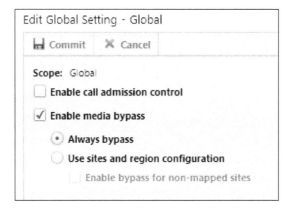

- Selecting **Use sites and region configuration** in the **Global** settings:
    - ° You can leverages region/sites definition
    - ° You can assign a Bypass ID to each site/region
    - ° Clients and gateways will receive a Bypass ID
    - ° If the Bypass ID matches, the media bypass feature is used

Both possible configurations (as we have seen in the previous screenshots) require the trunk to be enabled for media bypass:

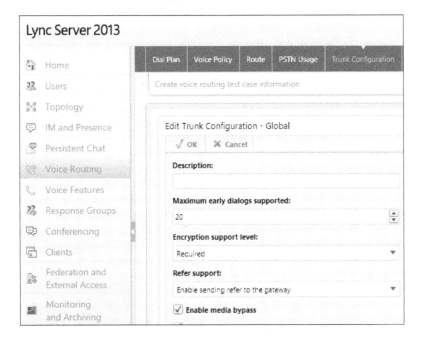

Media bypass (as the name states) helps us to avoid the need to pass through the Mediation server for the media traffic, not for the signaling traffic.

Call admission control (CAC)

Call admission control is a service built into the Lync Server. It limits the number of simultaneous calls and real-time connections, so the available bandwidth is managed, and the quality of the calls stays assured.

CAC is configured through the **New Bandwidth Policy** dialog; we then have to define the bandwidth limits in a dedicated policy as follows:

As we have seen, no special equipment is required to enforce CAC, and it supports control on audio, video, and conferencing.

The policy is based on the location of the client, so we are able to manage **quality of service (QOS)** in a dynamic manner, according to the changing connection point of our users. In Lync, it is necessary to define the subnets we use in our network in order to use this feature.

SIP trunk deployment

SIP trunking is a smart way for your Lync deployment to obtain telephone services from an external provider.

The trunk enables internal users to call the PSTN network, and allows external users to call Lync clients with a direct number.

The deployment of a SIP trunk does not require specific hardware (such as a PBX or a gateway) because it is based on a straight connection to a service provider.

It is also a great solution if you think to deploy Lync combined with an existing VoIP or telephonic solution and you do not want to use the existing voice services and numbers. This solution implies that your Mediation server has two network interfaces, one will be talking with the Front End Servers, and the other one will be connected to Edge of the service provider. You can set up a trunk from the Lync Management Shell or from the Lync Control Panel. The parameters will be dictated by the standard that is used from your provider.

Summary

Now that we have introduced the features of the Mediation server, we are ready to talk about the Enterprise Voice. The topics examined during this chapter will be useful during the next chapter, when we will see the fundamentals of the Lync voice.

5
Getting Started with Lync Enterprise Voice

In the previous chapter, we have talked about the Mediation Server, the fundamental role to enable your Lync users and infrastructure to talk with the public telephony systems and to connect with existing IP PBX. In this chapter, we will see all the steps and tools we need to manage Enterprise Voice.

Dial plans, voice policies, **public switched telephone network (PSTN)** usage records, and voice routes are the four basic configuration areas we have to set up if we want to use Enterprise Voice. However, the first configuration we usually meet is related to the user, and is called **direct inward dialing (DID)**.

Direct inward dialing

DID is a unique number, which we need to associate to a Lync user, every time we enable the **Enterprise Voice** option (as we can see in the following screenshot) or the conference features.

It is not a mandatory setting, but if a user does not have a DID number, he or she can only be reached through an internal extension.

 It is a best practice to also populate the **Active Directory** (**AD**) with phone numbers that are globally unique because Lync relies on the AD to provide a company-wide directory service.

The format of the Tel URI is dictated by the RFC 3966. The number used in the previous figure is a E.164 number, so we have the **+** sign, the **Country Code**, the **City / Area Code**, and the **Local (User) Number**. The result is a phone number that can be used to call the Lync user directly from a public/PSTN telephony system. The **Ext** parameter is a supported extension that we need for conferencing (for example, in dial-in conferencing to authenticate the user). To have a representation of the number, we can look at the following figure:

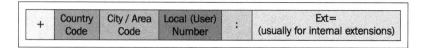

A globally unique valid DID needs no modification when the user calls an external number, as long as the gateway supports E.164 numbers. If our scenario is not the aforementioned one, we need to apply normalization rules, so that the number is communicated in the right manner. Normalization rules are also important to help users in composing telephone numbers with no need to use E.164 format. Another kind of number we are able to use is the local number that is not globally unique and requires an extension phone-context. The number will look similar to *111+a_string_*, and the format is the one you can see in the following figure, with no + sign, and an alphanumeric string that usually identifies a domain or a context.

Usually, local numbers are used when we have to interact with an existing third-party UC solution.

Internal extensions – users without DID

We have talked about the Ext parameter. Another possible use of this one is for situations where the user has no direct number available. In such a scenario, the number will be of a reachable type, and the extent will identify the single operator. So, to stay with the previous example, we would have user A with a line URI `tel:+18776967786;ext=1112`, and user B with a line URI `tel:+18776967786;ext=1113`. An additional step will be needed to keep the base number reachable, so we have to add a number `tel:+18776967786;ext=7786`, and make it usable through a normalization rule. The aforementioned number could be assigned to an operator who will receive the incoming calls, and also helps in forwarding them to the desired extension.

The method we have outlined here has some limits. A really good article *Lync Enterprise Voice Best Practices – Extensions* at `http://ucken.blogspot.it/2011/05/enterprise-voice-best-practices-in-lync.html` outlines some of them.

Dial plans

Dial plans are a set of translation rules used to convert the dialing habits of our company to the E.164 standard. The way our users compose a number is a mix of dialing public numbers and reaching internal extents. The aforementioned scenario means that dial plans will be tied to the story of the specific company.

Dial plans in the Lync Control Panel have a dedicated tab, which we can see in the following screenshot:

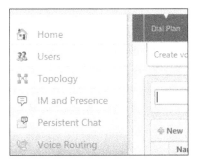

When we create a new rule, we can add associated normalization rules, as shown in the following screenshot:

Normalization rules are based on regular expressions, such as the following ones:

Regular Expression	Examples	Target String	Match
^ matches at the beginning of the string	^(187)	18776967786	187
\d matches any digit	\d	+18776967786	18776967786
\d{x} matches any x digits	(\d{3}\d+)	+18776967786	18776967786 requires the number to be at least 3-character long)
(x)|(y) x or y	(9)|(76)	+18776967786	9
[..] matches any character inside the brackets, with no particular order	[95]	+18776967786	9
(...) captures the enclosed characters for referring to them in the result as $1, $2, $3, and so on	^(999$\|112$)	999	999 is used for emergency numbers (for example, where the translation rule based on this regular expression could be +$1)

> A couple of good places to start learning about regular expressions are *Regular-Expressions.info* http://www.regular-expressions.info/reference.html, and *Tips on Understanding Microsoft Regular Expressions* http://images.globalknowledge.com/wwwimages/whitepaperpdf/WP_Parlas_MicrosoftOCS.pdf.

The normalization rule builder has four areas to configure:

- **Starting digits**: This area defines the leading digits of dialed numbers you want the pattern to match.
- **Length**: This area defines the number of digits in the matching pattern.
- **Digits to remove**: This area defines the number of starting digits to be removed from dialed numbers.
- **Digits to add**: This area defines the digits to be added to dialed numbers.

Manual editing and number testing are allowed, with the outline shown in the following screenshot:

A dial plan is applied to a scope, that could be user, pool, site, or global. As usual, the most specific policy will be applied over the other ones.

 There is a default normalization rule, to keep all the results for
`^(\d{11})$` that matches any 11-digit number. Often we have to
reconfigure it, because such a normalization will not fit most scenarios.

The preceding behavior is useful to address the need of the different branch offices, locations, and remote sites of our company. The main advantage of a user dial plan is that it will be applied consistently even if we have roaming of failover scenarios.

Off-hook dialing

Really often a telephone system user lifts the receiver off the hook, and then composes the number he/she wants to call (that is a normal behavior also with a Lync deskphone). A standard PBX will connect the user to the number, as soon as it has enough digits to dial a meaningful number. To avoid calling internal numbers if the first digits of the number we are going to call are the same of an internal telephone, we usually have a digit 9 to identify a call that is going out of the company. Lync has a similar feature, in the Dial plan, called External access prefix. This rule will not apply to a call on hook or from a client. For example, if there is an External access prefix 9 defined in a dial plan, any number dialed by the user with 9 as the first number will not be processed by the number normalization rule with internal extension checked in the dial plan.

Voice policies

Lync voice policies limit Enterprise Voice functionality available to users (Voice Policy Entitlements) and authorized types of calls (PSTN Usages).

The policies define the following for each user, site, or organization that is assigned the policy:

- A set of **Enterprise Voice** features that can be enabled or disabled
- A definition of authorized calls made by the PSTN usage records

Voice policies are configured after selecting a voice route in the **Voice Routing** section, as we can see in the following screenshot. The available scopes for every voice policy are **User**, **Site**, and **Global** (a default **Global** policy is created during the installation phase) with the logic we have already seen of the most specific policy that will be applied over the other ones.

The features we can configure in the policy are the ones we can see in the following screenshot:

The default situation is the one depicted in the previous screenshot: call forwarding, delegation, call transfer, simultaneous ringing, team call, and PSTN reroute enabled.

To understand the single voice feature, a good starting point is the TechNet documentation about voice policies at `http://technet.microsoft.com/en-us/library/gg412891.aspx`. PSTN usage records are a required part in every voice policy, and are applied in the order from top to bottom. As soon as a matching rule is found, it will be applied and the search will not go on.

PSTN usage records

PSTN usage records (we can find them in the **Voice Routing** tab) are used to create user profiles related to the call permissions. As we can see in the following screenshot, they are similar to an empty box, which we have to fill with voice routes.

PSTN usage records can comprise several associated routes, and can be assigned to different voice policies. The usage record will be usually related to a particular site or office. Finding a matching rule means that the user is allowed to call the number he or she dialed. As we said, we have to apply voice routes.

Voice routes

When a Lync user dials a phone number, we must match it with an object in E.164 format defined in Lync (such as a user, a call park orbit, or an unassigned number) or we need to have a corresponding voice route. If the aforementioned configuration is not true, we will have a SIP error 404, meaning a "No matching rule" in this scenario. Regular expressions (that we have already seen) are used also in voice routes to specify the numbers the route will apply using the following options:

- We can use the **Build a pattern to match** function to generate a regular expression
- Or we can write it manually

These options are shown in the following screenshot:

This way, we have created a voice route for the U.K. – London zone, and then typing the phone number, we have automatically applied the normalization rule.

The match tool allows two types of pattern matching: starting digits for numbers that you want to allow or exceptions. We can also select Suppress caller ID, if we want to hide the ID of the caller to the call recipient. We can refer to the following screenshot for creating a voice route.

Another mandatory element in a voice route is the associated trunk; that is, one or more gateways that enable us to give a path for the call to go outside our network. Voice gateways are defined in the Lync Topology Builder. In the Shared Components folder, we have the PSTN gateways folder. If we right-click on it, we are able to define a new gateway, as we can see in the following screenshot:

The configuration wizard will ask for some information about the gateway, and then after the procedure, it is ready to be published with the topology (and used in the voice routes), as we can see in the following screenshot (where we have defined a PSTN gateway named `PSTN_Outgoing`).

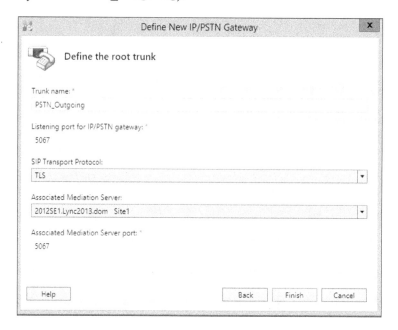

It is important to remark that gateway and Mediation Server association is defined only in the topology, and this is something fundamental to route the numbers outside our company.

The settings we define for the IP/PSTN gateway, depend on the requirements that different vendors have to connect with Lync, so consider the ones shown in the previous screenshot as an example.

Unassigned Numbers

Talking about voice routes, we have said that one of the objects, which we can use in Lync to manage calls, are the Unassigned Numbers. In Lync, we can define the numbers that are valid for our company but are not assigned. Incoming calls will be matched with a table containing the aforementioned numbers, and then can be redirected to an Announcement or to Exchange UM (if we have one). To manage unassigned numbers, we have to create a table containing all the valid numbers on our Lync system.

The call will be compared to the contents of the table only if there is no matching assigned number. So, it is a smart way to configure the Unassigned Numbers. To configure the announcement, we can use the Lync command line with a cmdlet as follows:

```
New-CSAnnouncement -Name "Voice Announcement" -TextToSpeechPrompt "This
number is not assigned at the moment" -Language "en-US" -Identity "servic
e:ApplicationServer:2012SE1.Lync2013.dom" -Verbose
```

It is also possible to import a pre-recorded audio file to the File Store by running the `Import-CsAnnouncementFile` cmdlet.

 Some examples of the use of the aforementioned cmdlet are available on Microsoft TechNet at `http://technet.microsoft.com/en-us/library/gg398472.aspx`.

Now, if we want to create a table with an unassigned number having extensions from `100` to `999`with a base number `+18776967000`, we can configure it by navigating to **Voice Features | Unassigned Number**, as shown in the following screenshot:

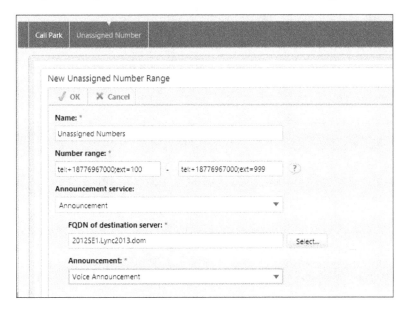

Call Park

With Call Park we are able to place a call on hold, and there it waits to be picked up from another telephone (using a virtual extension that will be automatically assigned to the call).

The base configuration (that we can see in the following screenshot) is made by navigating to **Voice Features** | **Call Park**, and it is really easy. The only important reminder is that the number range must use the * or # character.

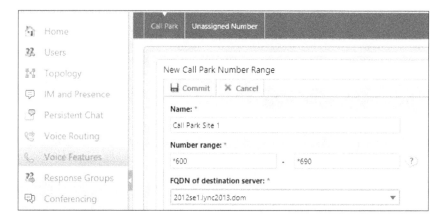

The logical process behind a call

In the following figure we have a synthesis of the concepts we have explained about **VOICE POLICIES**, **PSTN USAGE RECORDS**, and **VOICE ROUTES**. The process is to verify if a user is enabled to use a voice feature and to make the call, to define which type of call we are making, and then to route it to the PSTN, the PBX, or the gateway.

We can develop the preceding concept a little more, examining the different mechanisms that Lync uses for outgoing calls.

Every time we perform a reverse-number lookup on the phone number of the caller, (we check it to verify, if it matches one of the phone numbers on the caller's contact list, or in the **Global Address List** (**GAL**)). If the number is an internal one, the call will be forwarded to the number of our company that matches the call.

When the user initiates a call, the first evaluation is related to emergency numbers. If the call is an E9-1-1 call, it is immediately delivered to a **Location Policy** (a Lync **Location Policy** defines the settings for E9-1-1 during client registration). The emergency call at that point is moved to the **Voice Route**, and then sent to the destination.

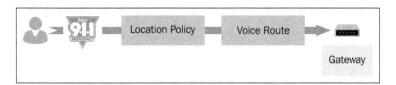

 Enhanced 911 (E911) is a system used in North America to link emergency callers with the appropriate public resources. Outside the United States and Canada, this type of facility is defined as caller location, and local rules may exist to ensure that the position of the caller dialing an emergency number is used.

A normal call passes through more steps, which are listed as follows:

1. The first control regards the format of the number and the destination. If it is already in a E.164 format, Lync will perform a **Number Lookup**.

2. If we have no match on our company numbers, call park, or vacant numbers, the second step is to pass the call to the policies (**Voice Policy** and **PSTN Usage**).

3. The final step is to apply the **Voice Route** to forward the call.

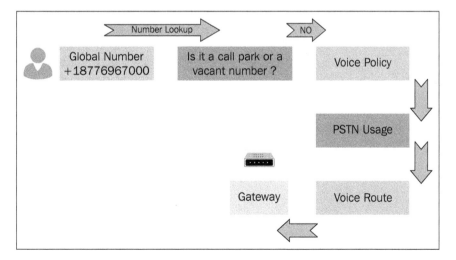

A call that is not for a **Global Number**, will also be normalized before the **Number Lookup** and the other steps we have seen for a **Global Number**. Normalization Rules are part of the dial plan.

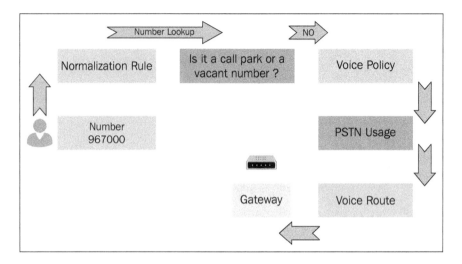

 An exception to all the aforementioned flows and controls is the case of a desk user who calls an SIP URI. In such a scenario, the call will be forwarded with no further processing.

Summary

Enterprise Voice is probably the most complex aspect of a Lync deployment. In this chapter, we have seen some basic concepts and tools to configure, and manage voice in Lync 2013 with some practical hints that should be really useful in day-to-day Lync administration. The next chapter focuses on an entire new role, the Persistent Chat Server. This is a powerful feature, often underrated, that can fit in many specific scenarios.

6
Deploying Persistent Chat Server

Persistent Chat Server is a new functionality of Lync 2013 (Lync Server 2010 had the group chat that was really different). Persistent Chat enables chat and IM conversations to be continued over time. Some of the more interesting new features related to Persistent Chat in Lync 2013 are the administrative interfaces integrated in the Lync Server Control Panel, the deployment managed through the Topology Builder, and the new solutions dedicated to high availability. Persistent Chat is a Lync role that can live by itself as a single server or as a dedicated pool, but the Persistent Chat Front End could also be collocated with a Lync Server 2013 Standard Edition.

Why Persistent Chat

The main advantage of the Persistent Chat Server over a normal mail communication is that the entire flow of conversation is always available. People who will take part in the conversation a second time have the opportunity to read all the information that has been exchanged. Persistent Chat is also powerful as a single reference point, where all the users interested in a certain project are sure to find the data they need. Scenarios such as brainstorming and sharing information between employees at different workplaces and working shifts are the best ones for such a feature.

Persistent Chat Server installation

As we said before, depending on your Lync deployment, the Chat Server has to be deployed as a dedicated pool (with Lync Enterprise Edition), or can be collocated (Lync Standard Edition). The Persistent Chat requires a dedicated instance on a database (mandatory in the first scenario), or could also be collocated on the local SQL Express (in the second situation). In our example, we will deploy the service on a Standard Edition Server, but the database will be on a separate SQL Server with a dedicated instance.

The following are the steps to be performed for installing the Persistent Chat Server:

1. The first step, as we can see, will be performed in the Topology Builder, which is defining a new Persistent Chat pool (the menu is the same even if we collocate the role).

2. In a Standard Edition scenario, the value of the **FQDN** field is the name of the Lync Front End Server, where Persistent Chat will be collocated (see the following screenshot):

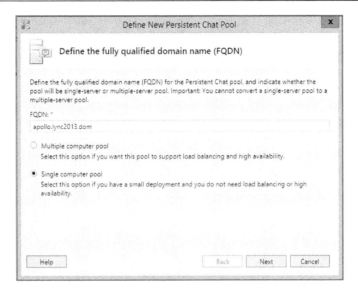

3. The following screenshot will require a display name that has no impact on the configuration. The compliance flag is important if our company needs to follow established guidelines, specifications, or legislations that require a record of our company's chat/IM activities. If we want to use this feature, a compliance service will be collocated on our Front End Server. The compliance feature also requires an additional database (`mgccomp`) that we can collocate in the SQL instance, where the Persistent Chat database (`mgc`) is installed (or in the SQL Express database of the Standard Edition Server, if we want to keep the number of servers as low as possible).

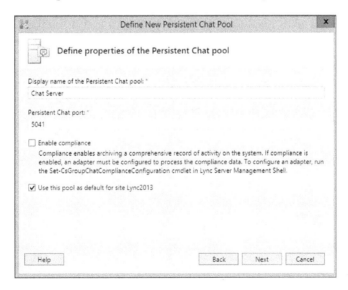

4. The wizard will then require to define the SQL Server Store. The next configuration is related to the file store (a copy of any file uploaded will be saved there). The user that is performing the configuration needs to have full control on the folder (the Topology Builder will need this kind of access to configure a set of permissions). It is mandatory for the path to be of a **Universal Naming Convention** (**UNC**) if we have more than one Persistent Chat Server, or else we can select a local path too. In the following screenshot, we have preferred to use a UNC, and also the folder is a local one.

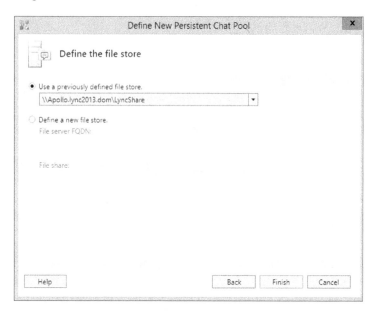

5. If we are happy with the configuration (in our example, the one shown in the screenshot), we will be able to publish the topology, as we have done in the previous chapters.

6. The Topology Builder will also create the Persistent Chat database, as shown in the following screenshot:

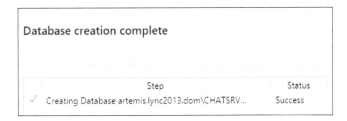

Managing categories, chat rooms, and privacy

All the conversations in Lync 2013 Persistent Chat are organized in "rooms". These rooms are known as chat rooms, and could be used as a logical separation between different topics and working groups. In every room, we will find messages, attachments, and information that have been added over time. Characteristics and management of the rooms are dictated by categories that we define through the administrative tools of Lync. The first mandatory step is to define a category as we can see in the following screenshot; this can be done using the Control Panel.

The following are the steps to be performed for managing chats, categories, and privacy:

1. The first step (shown in the following screenshot) is to select the chat service on which we are going to work (because we could have deployed more than one service or the Persistent Chat pool).

2. We are able to define a name for the category-related features such as invitations and uploads, and a list of members (allowed to participate in rooms of such a category) such as denied members (that will be excluded) and creators (that will be able to create rooms in the category, and in this way receive a sort of "delegation" in the management of Persistent Chat).

As you can see in the following screenshot, we have some options:

- **Enable invitations**: If this option is selected, rooms may or may not be allowed to have invitations; if cleared, the rooms are not allowed to have invitations.

- **Enable file upload**: If this option is selected, the rooms can enable or disable file uploads; if cleared, the rooms are allowed to have file uploads.

- **Enable chat history**: If this option is selected, room chats become non-persistent.

This is all we have to do in the administrative interface. The remaining part of the work is up to the user, connected from a "full" Lync client (the one included in the Office suite, as explained in *Chapter 7, Choosing Lync 2013 Clients*).

Users are able to search for rooms in categories where they are members. An exception is that the rooms are flagged as "secret" by the creator of the room. In such a scenario, only the users who are already members of the room will see the secret rooms in the search.

Now, we will create a whole new room, as shown in the following screenshot:

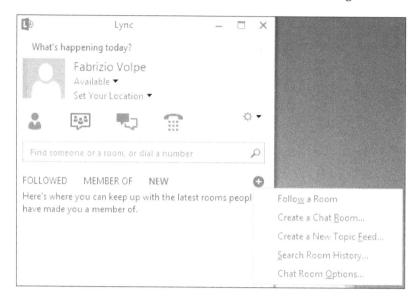

The following are the steps to be performed while creating a whole new room:

1. A web interface will be launched, and then the user will be able to generate a new room, as shown in the following screenshot:

2. The following screenshot shows the options available during the room's creation. The **Privacy** options will have an impact on the search and accessibility of the single room, as we have explained before.

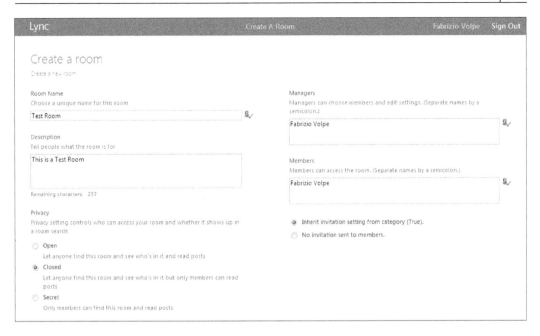

3. Now we are able to see a new room in the web interface.

4. The room will be shown in the client, and then we will be able to work inside it.

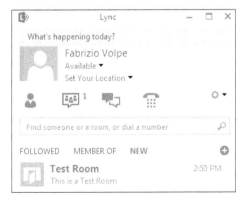

5. We will be able to interact in it by adding messages, documents, and so on, as we are able to see in the following screenshot:

Summary

As seen in this chapter, Persistent Chat Server is a good foundation on which we can build knowledge bases, and is really interesting when it comes to keeping information in an organized and easy-to-use form. The next chapter is focused on the clients. Lync offers a great deal of ways to access its services, and we will see all the available versions and solutions in order to give a flexible and straightforward interface to our users.

7
Choosing Lync 2013 Clients

Since March and April 2013, Lync 2013 mobile clients have been made available for iPhone, iPad, Windows Phone, and Android. Audio and video over IP are available with this release of the client, and this is something we have to keep in mind when we are planning our clients' deployment because the mobile version is now a viable alternative (if not a replacement) to the full Lync 2013 client.

What clients are available?

At the moment, we are writing a list that includes the following clients:

- Full client, as a part of Office 2013 Plus
- The Lync 2013 app for Windows 8
- Lync 2013 for mobile devices
- The Lync Basic 2013 version

 A plugin is needed to enable Lync features on a virtual desktop. We need the full Lync 2013 client installation to allow Lync access to the user.

Although they are not clients in the traditional sense of the word, our list must also include the following ones:

- The Microsoft Lync VDI 2013 plugin
- Lync Online (Office 365)
- Lync Web App
- Lync Phone Edition
- Legacy clients that are still supported (Lync 2010, Lync 2010 Attendant, and Lync 2010 Mobile)

Full client (Office 2013)

This is the most complete client available at the moment. It includes full support for voice, video, IM (similarly to the previous versions), and integration for the new features (for example, high-definition video, the gallery feature to see multiple video feeds at the same time, and chat room integration). In the following screenshot, we can see a tabbed conversation in Lync 2013:

Its integration with Office implies that the group policies for Lync are now part of the Office group policy's administrative templates. We have to download the Office 2013 templates from the Microsoft site and install the package in order to use them (some of the settings are shown in the following screenshot):

Lync is available with the Professional Plus version of Office 2013 (and with some Office 365 subscriptions).

Lync 2013 app for Windows 8

The Lync 2013 app for Windows 8 (also called Lync Windows Store app) has been designed and optimized for devices with a touchscreen (with Windows 8 and Windows RT as operating systems). The app (as we can see in the following screenshot) is focused on images and pictures, so we have a tile for each contact we want in our favorites.

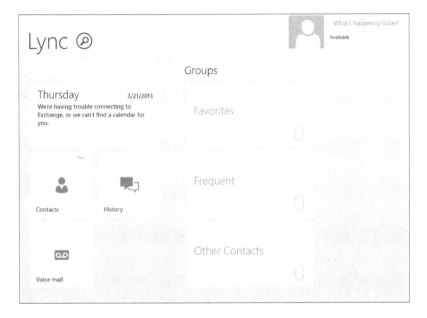

The Lync Windows Store app supports contact management, conversations, and calls, but some features such as Persistent Chat and the advanced management of Enterprise Voice, are still an exclusive of the full client.

Also, talking about conferencing, we will not be able to act as the presenter or manage other participants. The app is integrated with Windows 8, so we are able to use **Search** to look for Lync contacts (as shown in the following screenshot):

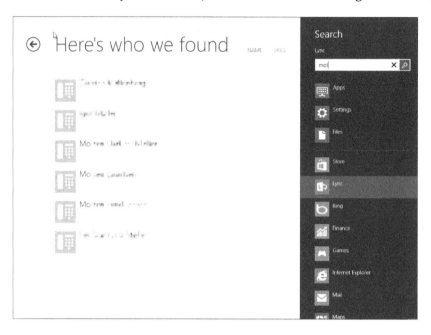

Lync 2013 for mobile devices

The Lync 2013 client for mobile devices is the solution Microsoft offers for the most common tablet and smartphone systems (excluding those tablets using Windows 8 and Windows RT with their dedicated app). It is available for Windows phones, iPad/iPhone, and for Android. The older version of this client was basically an IM application, and that is something that somehow limited the interest in the mobile versions of Lync. The 2013 version that we are talking about includes support for VOIP and video (using Wi-Fi networks and cellular data networks), meetings, and for voice mail. From an infrastructural point of view, enabling the new mobile client means to apply the Lync 2013 Cumulative Update 1 (CU1) on our Front End and Edge servers and publish a DNS record (lyncdiscover) on our public name servers. If we have had previous experience with Lync 2010 mobility, the difference is really noticeable. The lyncdiscover record must be pointed to the reverse proxy. Reverse proxy deployment requires for a product to be enabled to support Lync mobility, and a certificate with the lyncdiscover's public domain name needs to be included.

As we have seen in *Chapter 1, Installing a Lync 2013 Enterprise Pool*, the Wildcards SSL certificate is not recommended, and this is valid also on the reverse proxy in association with lyncdiscover (the other web services could work).

Lync Basic 2013 version

Lync Basic 2013 is a downloadable client that provides basic functionalities. It does not provide support for advanced call features, multiparty videos or galleries, and skill-based searches. Lync Basic 2013 is dedicated to companies with Lync 2013 on-premises, and it is for Office 365 customers that do not have the full client included with their subscription. A client will look really similar to the full one, but the display name on top is **Lync Basic** as we can see in the following screenshot:

Microsoft Lync VDI 2013 plugin

As we said before, the VDI plugin is not a client; it is software we need to install to enable Lync on virtual desktops based on the most used technologies, such as Microsoft RDS, VMware View, and XenDesktop. The main challenge of a VDI scenario is granting the same features and quality we expect from a deployment on a physical machine. The plugin uses "Media Redirection", so that audio and video originate and terminate on the plugin running on the thin client. The user is enabled to connect conferencing/telephony hardware (for example microphones, cams, and so on) to the local terminal and use the Lync 2013 client installed on the virtual desktop as it was running locally. The plugin is the only Lync software installed at the end-user workplace. The details of the deployment (*Deploying the Lync VDI Plug-in*) are available at `http://technet.microsoft.com/en-us/library/jj204683.aspx`.

Citrix has released a different solution called the Citrix HDX Optimization Pack for Microsoft Lync that introduces an additional Citrix UI and disables native Lync audio and video for VDI users. The main advantage of this solution is that the aforementioned software is installed on the virtual desktop, while the software to connect to the VDI is the receiver, which is available for a great number of operating systems and devices. Using the Optimization Pack, you will receive a message like the one you can see in the following screenshot:

At the moment, we are writing that the solution is available for a Lync 2010 client, and a dedicated version of Lync 2013 will be available in the coming days. See the *Support for Lync 2013: DVC Implementation Versus the Citrix HDX Optimization Pack for Microsoft Lync* page at `http://blogs.technet.com/b/nexthop/ archive/2012/12/21/support-for-lync-2013-dvc-implementation-vs-the- citrix-hdx-optimization-pack-for-microsoft-lync.aspx`.

Lync Online (Office 365)

Lync, as part of the Office 365 offer, works similar to a full client with an important exception: Enterprise Voice. If we want to enable our users to access the aforementioned feature, we have to design a hybrid deployment (split domain) with a voice feature that will be granted only to on-premises users. The split domain solution enables us to have a single domain name for both the environments, and move users from on-premises to online deployment based on the features they need. It is strongly suggested that you have all the workloads of a user moved accordingly so online users have the best experience using Exchange Online and SharePoint Online, and vice versa.

Lync Web App

The Lync Web App is a web application based on HTML and JavaScript that enables users that have no client software installed locally to participate in a Lync meeting. It supports audio, video, and sharing with a simplified interface that has been designed to accommodate all the meeting needs of a guest. The screenshot that follows shows a meeting as seen by a Web App user. Part of the features we usually associate with the full client are also available in this interface.

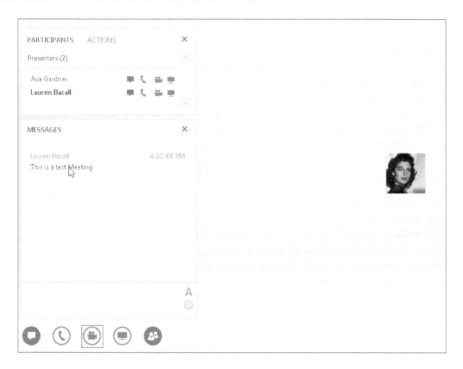

A user that tries to join a meeting using the Lync Web App for the first time will be required to download a plugin that supports Internet Explorer 8, 9, and 10, Firefox 12, Safari 5, and Chrome 18 (the last two are really important for compatibility with Mac OS X clients). The complete list is available on the TechNet *Lync Web App Supported Platforms* page at http://technet.microsoft.com/en-us/library/gg425820.aspx.

In the following screenshot, we are able to see the launch screen for a user accessing the Lync Web App.

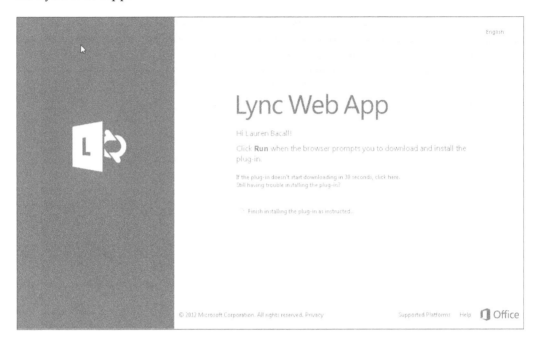

The Web App also supports multifactor authentication. We may require additional authentication, such as smart cards or PINs, to authenticate external users when they sign in to Lync meetings.

 For additional information, we can view the TechNet *Deploying Lync Web App* page at `http://technet.microsoft.com/ en-us/library/jj205190(v=ocs.15).aspx`.

If a user endpoint has a Lync client available locally, a web page will launch the meeting inside the client. We are able to configure the meeting page so that the legacy versions of the client are also supported (see *Chapter 3, Deploying Lync Mobility*).

Lync Phone Edition

Lync Phone Edition is a dedicated version of the Lync software that has been optimized for unified communication devices. (The term has been used here to refer mainly to phones running Lync Phone Edition as their way to connect to Lync Server.) The aforementioned category includes desk phones (handsets or USB devices), conferencing (designed for use in a meeting room), and common area phones (to be used in public areas). In the following image, we can see some of the peripherals included in the list:

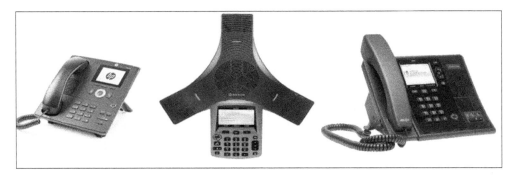

Microsoft considers two categories: phones compatible with Lync 2013 and phones optimized for Lync 2013 (the *IP Phones* page at `http://technet.microsoft.com/en-us/lync/gg278172.aspx`). The base difference is that compatible IP phones run manufacturer OSes while those optimized for Lync IP phones are powered by Lync Phone Edition.

Legacy clients

If we have an existing Lync 2010 deployment, existing clients will be able to work with Lync 2013. A special situation arose with Lync 2010 Attendee, a minimal client that was deployed to meet participants with no pre-existing local installation. The Web App that we have seen before completely replaces and surpasses what we were able to do with Attendee. Lync 2010 Attendant (a software designed for receptionists and people who have to manage and route a high number of calls) is still supported with Lync 2013, but has not been replaced with a new client at the moment.

We can get an idea of the work it has been optimized for from the following screenshot:

The official document *Client Interoperability in Lync 2013* is available at `http://technet.microsoft.com/en-us/library/jj204672.aspx`. If we want to allow or deny access to our system to just one version of the client we will be able to manage it using the client policies of Lync.

Summary

We have seen a short list of the clients available in Lync 2013. The extreme variety and flexibility that Lync delivers to the end user, paired with a really friendly and intuitive interface, is without doubt one of the strong aspects of Lync and often gives it an advantage over other UC solutions. Deploying the right client is a really fundamental part of a successful Lync implementation.

Index

Lync Server Backup Service 44
Lync Server roles
  about 5, 6
  additional servers, for external
      user access 6
  areas, archiving 7
  areas, director 7
  areas, mediation 7
  areas, monitoring 7
  areas, Persistent Chat Server 7
  Lync Edge 6
  reverse proxy 7, 8
Lync services. *See* AutodiscoverServices
Lync Web App 99

M

media bypass
  about 63
  configuring, ways 64, 65
  deploying 63
Mediation server
  collocated server, configuring 60, 61
  configuring 60
  improvements, in Lync 2013 63
  tasks 62
Mediation server configuration
  about 60, 61
  standalone server, configuring 61
Mediation server improvements, in Lync
    2013
  Caller ID 63
  Hybrid voice 63
  Inter-trunk routing 63
  M:N trunk routing 63
meet, URL 15
Microsoft Lync VDI 2013 plugin 97

N

NAT 55
Network Address Translation. *See* NAT
New Bandwidth Policy dialog 66
normal call
  steps 81
Number Lookup 82

O

off-hook dialing 74

P

Persistent Chat Server
  about 83
  installing 84
Persistent Chat Server installation
  about 84
  categories, managing 87
  chat rooms, managing 87
  privacy, managing 87
  steps 84-86
Physical pools 44
Planning Tool 9
pool 8
privacy
  managing 88, 89
Privacy options 90
PSTN 69
PSTN usage records 76
public switched telephone network.
      See PSTN
push notification configuration 57, 58

Q

quality of service (QOS) 66

R

reverse proxy 51

S

SANs 18
SE 5
Search 96
server failures
  managing 45
SIP trunking deployment 66, 67
SQL mirroring 9
SSL digital certificate 52
Standard Edition server. *See* SE
Subject Alternative Names. *See* SANs

T

Topology Builder
  checklist 20, 21

U

UAG 51
UNC 86
Unified Communication (UC) 18
Universal Naming Convention. *See* UNC
user groups 42

V

voice policies 74, 75
voice routes
  about 76-78, 81
  Call Park 79
  unassigned Numbers 78

W

Windows 8
  Lync 2013 app 95
Windows Fabric 43
Windows Fabric component 42

Thank you for buying
Getting Started with Microsoft Lync Server 2013

About Packt Publishing

Packt, pronounced 'packed', published its first book "Mastering phpMyAdmin for Effective MySQL Management" in April 2004 and subsequently continued to specialize in publishing highly focused books on specific technologies and solutions.

Our books and publications share the experiences of your fellow IT professionals in adapting and customizing today's systems, applications, and frameworks. Our solution based books give you the knowledge and power to customize the software and technologies you're using to get the job done. Packt books are more specific and less general than the IT books you have seen in the past. Our unique business model allows us to bring you more focused information, giving you more of what you need to know, and less of what you don't.

Packt is a modern, yet unique publishing company, which focuses on producing quality, cutting-edge books for communities of developers, administrators, and newbies alike. For more information, please visit our website: www.packtpub.com.

About Packt Enterprise

In 2010, Packt launched two new brands, Packt Enterprise and Packt Open Source, in order to continue its focus on specialization. This book is part of the Packt Enterprise brand, home to books published on enterprise software – software created by major vendors, including (but not limited to) IBM, Microsoft and Oracle, often for use in other corporations. Its titles will offer information relevant to a range of users of this software, including administrators, developers, architects, and end users.

Writing for Packt

We welcome all inquiries from people who are interested in authoring. Book proposals should be sent to author@packtpub.com. If your book idea is still at an early stage and you would like to discuss it first before writing a formal book proposal, contact us; one of our commissioning editors will get in touch with you.

We're not just looking for published authors; if you have strong technical skills but no writing experience, our experienced editors can help you develop a writing career, or simply get some additional reward for your expertise.

Microsoft Lync 2013 Unified
Communications: From
Telephony to Real-time
Communication in the Digital Age

Complete coverage of all issues for a unified
communications strategy

Daniel Jonathan Valik

[PACKT] enterprise

Microsoft Lync 2013 Unified Communications: From Telephony to Real Time Communication in the Digital Age

ISBN: 978-1-84968-506-1 Paperback: 224 pages

Complete coverage of all topics for a unified communications strategy

1. A real business case and example project showing you how you can optimize costs and improve your competitive advantage with a Unified Communications project

2. The book combines both business and the latest relevant technical information so it is a great reference for business stakeholders, IT decision makers, and UC technical experts

(MCTS): Microsoft BizTalk Server 2010
(70-595) Certification Guide

Johan Hedberg   Kent Weare
Morten la Cour   [PACKT] enterprise

(MCTS): Microsoft BizTalk Server 2010 (70-595) Certification Guide

ISBN: 978-1-84968-492-7 Paperback: 476 pages

A compact certification guid to help you prepare for and pass exam 70-595: TS Developing Business Process and Integration Solutions by using Microsoft BizTalk Servert 2010

1. This book and e-book will provide all that you need to know in order to pass the (70-595) Developing Business Process and Integration Solutions exam by Using Microsoft BizTalk Server 2010 book

2. Includes a comprehensive set of test questions and answers that will prepare you for the actual exam.

Please check **www.PacktPub.com** for information on our titles

Oracle ADF Enterprise Application Development—Made Simple

Oracle ADF Enterprise Application Development—Made Simple

Successfully plan, develop, test, and deploy enterprise applications with Oracle ADF

Sten E. Vesterli

Oracle ADF Enterprise Application Development—Made Simple

ISBN: 978-1-84968-188-9   Paperback: 396 pages

Successfully plan, develope, test, and deploy enterprise applications with Oracle ADF

1. Best practices for real-life enterprise application development

2. Proven project methodology to ensure success with your ADF project from an Oracle ACE Director

3. Understand the effort involved in building an ADF application from scratch, or converting an existing application

iPhone with Microsoft Exchange Server 2010: Business Integration and Deployment

Set up Microsoft Exchange Server 2010 and deploy iPhone and other iDevices securely into your business

Steve Goodman

iPhone with Microsoft Exchange Server 2010: Business Integration and Deployment

ISBN: 978-1-84969-148-2   Paperback: 290 pages

Set up Micrisoft Exchange Server 2010 and deploy iPhone and other iDevices security into your bussiness

1. Learn about Apple's mobile devices and how they work with Exchange Server 2010

2. Plan and deploy a highly available Exchange organization and Office 365 tenant

3. Create and enforce security policies and set up certificate-based authentication

Please check **www.PacktPub.com** for information on our titles

www.ingramcontent.com/pod-product-compliance
Lightning Source LLC
LaVergne TN
LVHW081346050326
832903LV00024B/1349